CRIME AND THE DEVELOPMENT OF MODERN SOCIETY

Crime and the Development of Modern Society

PATTERNS OF CRIMINALITY IN NINETEENTH CENTURY GERMANY AND FRANCE

HOWARD ZEHR

CROOM HELM
ROWMAN AND LITTLEFIELD

First published 1976
© 1976 Howard Zehr

Croom Helm Ltd, 2-10 St John's Road, London SW11

ISBN 0-85664-235-5

First published in the United States 1976
by Rowman and Littlefield, Totowa, New Jersey

Library of Congress Cataloging in Publication Data

Zehr, Howard.
    Crime and the development of modern society.

    Bibliography: p. 177
    1. Crime and criminals—Germany—History. 2. Crime and criminals —
    France History. 3. Social history—19th century. I. Title.
HV6974.Z43 1976   364'.943   76-19109

ISBN 0-87471-861-9

Printed in Great Britain by Biddles Ltd, Guildford, Surrey

CONTENTS

PREFACE

In spite of the cold, impersonal facade of quantitative analysis, my interest in crime is by no means strictly academic. In fact, my concern with history generally is rather personal. This is not to say, of course, that I do not favour attempting objectivity; this we must all do, though I must admit some pessimism about the possibility of attaining that ideal. I mean, rather, that my reasons for studying history, and my reactions to history, are related directly to my concerns about myself and the world I live in. I believe that the reader has the right to such knowledge about an author, for even the most 'scientific' of cliometricians cannot eradicate the effects of biases and predilections from his work, and this is especially true when dealing with a subject as emotionally laden as crime.

And I did begin this study with certain attitudes about crime. Some of them I am aware of; others, unfortunately, I am not. I do know that I began with a great deal of concern for the situation of the offender. My research, as well as contacts and friendships with offenders, has only strengthened that attitude. This may have affected the types of interpretations I was willing to consider. At the very least, it has led me to deal with crime as neutrally as I could; I have, for instance, tried to avoid the prejudicial word 'criminal', replacing it with more relativistic terms such as 'offender' and 'delinquent' in order to emphasise the role of society as well as of those whom society terms 'criminal'. Similarly, I began with a number of assumptions and hypotheses about crime. Some of these, such as those discussed in the postscript, I have held to or modified slightly while others I have had to give up; some of my findings surprised me, other did not. Nevertheless, I think it is worth saying that I did not begin with a full-blown model to be tested. While I naturally have had to test certain hypotheses in the course of this study, my overall approach has approximated the one more widely accepted in the historical tradition, that of isolating what seemed to be patterns in the data and then finding reasonable explanations that fit. A case can be made for both types of approaches, of course, but the need for purely descriptive material on nineteenth-century criminality suggested the usefulness of the latter approach.

My deepest appreciation must go to Professor Stearns, who, first as my Ph.D. adviser, then as editor, spent hours carefully and patiently guiding me through this project. Similar feelings go to my family, who put up with me through this period. Unfortunately, it is impossible to acknowledge all of the other people and organisations which have given me assistance. Professors Seth M. Scheiner, Harry C. Bredemeier and Harold Poor read my manuscript at the dissertation stage and offered helpful suggestions. The Foreign Area Fellowship Program, the Southern Fellowships Fund, the Danforth Graduate Fellowship Program, and Talladega College all provided grants which made the research and writing possible. Rutgers University, Talladega College and Goshen College each made computer time available. Professor Rudolph M. Bell of Rutgers University as well as Professors Jerry Breecher and James L. Boettler of Talladega College answered many questions about my computer programs. I appreciate too the help provided by the personnel of numerous archives and libraries both in this country and in Europe, including especially the archives of the Prefecture of Police in Paris where I spent a great deal of time.

Needless to say, I bear sole responsibility for all statements and conclusions that follow.

1 INTRODUCTION

In 1895 Emile Durkheim made the startling observation that crime is normal in a society, 'an integral part of all healthy societies.'[1] This view was novel then and it is still all-too-novel now, although recent concern about violence in America and elsewhere has brought an increasing awareness of the continuity of disorder in our own history.

The tardiness of this awakening is unfortunate. Delinquent behaviour must be considered normal to a society for reasons that by now are becoming obvious. As far as we know, no modern society exists which is crimeless. Moreover, numerous studies have demonstrated that most of us, regardless of our social standing, are involved in delinquent behaviour at some point in our lives.[2] Crime, like the poor, is apparently always with us. But Durkheim went farther than this, arguing that crime should be considered normal because it plays a useful role in the integration of a society. Delinquent behaviour, he suggested, is boundary-maintaining: by injuring public morality, the offender draws the community together in indignation, thereby fostering social unity and helping the community to define and affirm a common morality and identity.[3] Later commentators have suggested other possibilities; some suggest for instance, that criminal behaviour is a form of social adaptation, representing an attempt to adjust to social norms, albeit in socially illegitimate ways. However, regardless of whether or not it is functional, the point is clear: crime, like sex and disease, is not an occasional aberration but a usual occurrence in human experience and as such deserves the attention of historians as well as that of criminologists. Although our knowledge is admittedly still incomplete, historical literature abounds with information about such everyday matters as birth, marriage and ploughing methods. Occasional outbreaks of collective violence — riots, revolutions, mass protests — have received even more attention. But surprisingly little is known about past patterns of criminal behaviour. It is high time that the more mundane forms of disorder received their due. For only through historical analysis can we develop a conceptual analysis of the relationship of crime to broader social processes such as industrialisation, and through this more than a superficial assessment even of present crime trends.

The Issues

This study, then deals with the history of crime — or, to put it another way, with crime as social history — in Germany and France during the nineteenth century. It does not, however, concern itself with the particular motives and situations of individual offenders. Nor does it report the fascinating details of crimes and trials. It records, instead, the results of an analysis of gross statistical patterns of crime for rather large geographic areas over long periods of time. In the parlance of the cliometricians, this is a quantitative study on the macro-level. That such an approach is taken is not meant to imply that closer case histories are unnecessary or illegitimate forms of history; these approaches are in fact desperately needed. Rather, the present approach was adopted in the belief that an analysis of this sort was a necessary first step to an understanding of the crime phenomenon. For in spite of many attempts, both quantitative and otherwise, to explore historical patterns of crime, surprisingly little is known about the behaviour of past crime rates and their overall causes. Did crime rise or fall during the past century? Were rates lower in the nineteenth century than later? Which areas had the highest rates? Which the lowest? In what periods were crime rates especially high? Such questions are by no means new. Indeed, they were raised by A.M. Guerry, often considered the founder of modern criminal science, as early as 1833 and they have been widely discussed since then, but the results have been rather contradictory and unconvincing, due, in many cases, to imprecise methods or indexes and to uncritical attitudes towards sources.[4] Until such basic questions as whether the incidence of crime increased or decreased during the century are answered, we can say little about the causes and meaning of crime.

Thus the first task is strictly empirical and requires the construction of usable and reliable indexes of crime. To this end, some new materials and methods will be used and, more importantly, attention will be given to deficiencies in crime records; if distortions in crime statistics cannot always be eliminated, they can at least be recognised and minimised. Only after this descriptive work is done can we move to issues of a more analytical nature. Three specific problems provide the focus here. None of them is new, but each merits further attention because of the tenuous and contradictory nature of many earlier conclusions. Moreover, in each case, if satisfactory answers to the questions can be suggested, important insights into nineteenth-century society — as well as into the the nature and significance of criminal behaviour — may be gained.

The relationship between crime and economic conditions serves as one basic focus. Did crime rise in periods of depression? Did crime decrease with prosperity and rising standards of living? The world-wide depression of the 1970s makes these questions especially pertinent, but the issue is old and has been debated heatedly. Because the issue is both important and controversial, therefore, it merits further investigation using more varied and precise indexes and methods than have usually been employed.

The second and third problems get at some of Western man's most basic assumptions and prejudices about both crime and modernity. Everyone knows that crime is more frequent today than it was in the stable rural milieu of our grandparents and great grandparents. In fact, many would argue, such a trend is inevitable. Modernity implies a decline in respect for conventions, a reduction in social controls, a lessening of appreciation for the rights and property of others. What could be more logical than that delinquency should accompany the modernisation process? Moreover, the growth of cities is usually considered a major catalyst in this development, for during the past century popular opinion, nourished by studies which were frequently biased against the city in favour of a nostalgic view of a lost rural paradise, has associated urban life with high crime rates. The city, in the popular view, is characterised by instability, impersonal relationships, social disorganisation and weakened social controls; it is the paradigm of modern society. Consequently the city is also characterised by high rates of delinquency and the urbanisation process, which dissolves the more stable traditions of the countryside, results in crime.

These assumptions are deeply ingrained in us, even when the most liberal contemplate a trip to New York or London's East End, but recent theory and research in various parts of the world is undermining many of them. Thus our second two questions are especially relevant here. First, were there in fact urban and rural differentials in nineteenth-century criminal behaviour; that is, can specifically rural and urban patterns of crime be isolated? Is crime really more common in the city than in the countryside and is it different in type? The second question is closely related to the first. What, if any, relationship existed between patterns of delinquency and the social upheaval which accompanied industrialisation and urbanisation? In the current terminology of the social sciences, what connection may be seen between criminality and the modernisation process? This latter question has in turn two dimensions. The most obvious, of course, is whether the social upheavals of the period led to increased crime as many assume. Just as important, however, is the question of whether patterns of criminal activity changed along with the modernisation of society. Did new types of criminal behaviour emerge, paralleling the modernisation of social relationships and values? The question of modernisation, then, is not simply whether social change led to increased crime via a break-down of social controls and traditions (or by some other mechanism), but also whether more modern values and patterns of behaviour are reflected in delinquent behaviour, that is, whether the nature of crime and its probable motives changed regardless of rate.

Nineteenth-century Germany and France provide an excellent context for the examination of these questions.[5] Between 1830 and 1914 both countries experienced substantial urbanisation and industrialisation. The rise of large cities and of large-scale, mechanised industry represented a significant break with the past and, in many cases, a massive disruption of traditional structures, values and routines. Centuries-old methods of production were abandoned and replaced by newer, more modern methods. Machines often took the place of manual labour, thereby displacing many persons and altering required work skills as well as the pace of work itself; although domestic industry survived well into the nineteenth century and even was temporarily boosted by rising demand in some instances, the characteristic work arena shifted from the family and small artisanal shop to the large factory where numerous workers, aided by machines, laboured under strict supervision. Populations grew rapidly. Increasing numbers of the rural population, pushed by the lack of jobs and land in the country-side or pulled by the lure of opportunities in the city, moved into new urban surroundings to seek work in factories and mills which were located there. Consequently, during the nineteenth century the percentage of the population which resided in urban areas in these two countries increased greatly; cities of unprecedented size arose; and the industrial city was born. Although standards of living generally rose in the long run, they fell for some elements of the population — especially at first — and were subject to frequent fluctuations: the nineteenth century was punctuated with economic crises of varying intensity which brought danger of actual starvation to some of the population and meant, at the very least, uncertainty for others. Hundreds of thousands of people were affected by these phenomena, many adversely, and even where actual change or hardship was not experienced, the threat of change itself caused fear and discontent. Both Germany and France, in other words, proved an important testing ground for the impact of the industrial revolution on crime.

Despite the difficulties involved, and in contrast to most historical studies undertaken, it was essential to adopt a comparative approach to answer the three questions we are addressing. Statistics from a single place and period are often quite uninformative and even misleading; it is only through comparisons among patterns in a variety of situations that significant and convincing conclusions are possible. We have seen claims, for example, that crime declined in England as industry matured. This is in fact debatable, but the larger point is that, dealing only with one, possibly special case, such claims tell us nothing about general relationships between crime and modern social change.[6] Here is where Germany and France provide important correctives from the comparative standpoint. The two nations shared common experiences during industrialisation and urbanisation in the nineteenth century: both nations underwent substantial social and economic changes, the populations of both were affected by severe economic fluctuations, and a significant proportion of both populations lived in cities by the latter part of the century. Moreover, both participated in the same Western cultural system and therefore cultural differences, although significant enough to be interesting, are not overwhelming. Yet, upon closer examination, the differences between the two countries are many. France began the process of industrialisation and urbanisation earlier than did Germany, yet proceeded much more slowly and was less completely transformed by 1914.[7] Conversely, the process began later but was telescoped into a shorter period in Germany. Heavy industry was more important in German industrialisation than in French, a factor which directly affected the extent of urban and industrial concentration and the nature of the working class. In spite of rapid and massive urbanisation, however, rural residence for some industrial workers persisted longer in Germany than in France due, in part, to a well-developed railway system. The role of the Government in stimulating industry, and also in controlling as well as protecting workers, was more pronounced in Germany than in France. Likewise, there were significant differences in working conditions, labour agitation, and in the size and efficiency of repressive apparatuses in the two countries.

Such differences, in spite of basic similarities, make these two national units particularly useful for comparative purposes. But for several reasons great care must be exercised when comparing national units. For one thing, differences in legal, judicial, and repressive systems complicate comparisons. Thus, while comparisons of trends in crime in the two countries are possible, variables such as how crimes were defined, what evidence was required for reporting or arrest, or how crimes were actually recorded make some international comparisons of crime levels tentative at best. Secondly, not all areas within either country shared similar experiences. Some regions in both Germany and France, such as the Ruhr area in Germany and the Nord and Pas-de-Calais in France, industrialised massively and rapidly during the century while other areas such as East Prussia or the Finistère were virtually untouched by these processes. Thus simple national comparisons may obscure important regional differences.

This raises one further issue which must be considered, if only secondarily. The regional diversity of these countries, noted above, suggests that the value of national rates as indicators of criminal patterns needs to be tested. Even though most questions are framed, and answered, on a national level in this analysis, we also test the extent to which national rates actually provide useful information about the incidence of delinquency. Of course, national rates may actually reflect behaviour which is distinctly national in character, attributable to culture or other shared experiences; German patterns of delinquency may be different from French. On the other hand, though, such rates may be purely mathematical averages of quite disparate regional or local patterns; this would be true, to return to a vital question raised earlier, if urban or rural patterns transcend national boundaries. National rates thus only have meaning if regional rates tend to be grouped around the national mean; if local rates are highly dispersed, national averages are at best mathematical abstractions. Fortunately, Germany and France in the nineteenth century also provide ample smaller regions where similarities and contrasts may be tested on a comparative basis.

The Data

A failure to recognise the significance of delinquency has not been the only cause for the neglect of crime in historical literature. Social historians have also avoided the subject of crime due to a deep distrust of crime statistics. Such suspicion is not entirely unwarranted; indeed, anyone acquainted with the controversies generated by the FBI's soaring index of crime in America cannot help but question the validity of crime records. Deficiences in FBI figures are only partially due to inadequacies inherent in the records themselves: crime statistics, like most statistical indexes, offer innumerable possibilities for misinterpretation and misuse. Nevertheless, obvious shortcomings in contemporary crime records have caused many social scientists to regard any attempt to study crime rates in the past as futile.[8]

The biases and distortions in crime records must not be glossed over. However, a close study of various crime indexes from both the nineteenth and twentieth centuries indicates that nineteenth-century criminal statistics are more plentiful and provide better indexes of delinquent behaviour than is commonly assumed.[9] Crime indexes are not random variables; records from the nineteenth century yield recurrent and comprehensible patterns of crime which cannot be attributed simply to biases in the records or to the activities of the agencies which compiled them. However, indexes must be carefully selected and constructed, and a recognition of basic distortions is essential.

The pros and cons of historical crime records need not be surveyed in detail here, but several guidelines for the use of crime records can be noted. Modern scholars are fairly well agreed that police statistics — and especially records of crimes made known to police as opposed to more arbitrary statistics of persons arrested — provide the best indexes of delinquency because they eliminate fewer crimes (the so-called 'dark figure') than any other category of record. Although it is often assumed that such statistics are lacking for the nineteenth century, a search of archival materials has turned up usable police statistics in some surprising places (e.g. in city administrative reports). Nevertheless, in practice a compromise is often necessary; most European governments opted for court records during the nineteenth century and thus a large body of well-organised and carefully collected court data is available on a national basis while police indexes are diverse and localised. Fortunately, comparisons of court and police data suggest that for some purposes court records may not be as bad a source as might be expected, so long as certain qualifications are recognised. Most importantly, the dark figure in nineteenth-century court records was not only larger than for police records, but also for certain property crimes such as theft it increased during the course of the century due, at least in part, to the failure of law enforcement agencies to expand as rapidly as population and crime levels and also, perhaps, to a decreasing emphasis upon the sanctity of private property which may have accompanied the urbanisation process.[10] Thus not only do court records significantly underestimate actual levels of crimes, but trends in theft rates based upon court records are much too negative, causing increases in theft rates to be underestimated or even ignored altogether.[11]

A second caution is that actual crime categories to be examined must be selected discriminately. Many crimes, by their nature, result in poor indexes. Sex crimes (where the victim may be embarrassed), very minor offences (where the offence is too small to bother with or where the police are not effective enough to make a report worth while) or arson (where, in the absence of a suspect, it is difficult to determine whether a crime actually occurred) are examples of crimes for which statistics are virtually worthless. These crimes are rarely reported and even more rarely result in arrest and trial. In general, records of crimes are considered to be better the more serious the offence and the more likely it is to involve a third party other than the offender and victim. Homicides, serious cases of assault and battery or theft, and bank robbery are examples of crimes for which indexes are considered relatively reliable.

Certain crimes, in other words, are almost impossible to study by using traditional sources.[12] Moreover, the use of general indexes of crime — such as total crime or total crimes against persons and property — is practically ruled out. General groupings of crime can give exceedingly misleading results because rates are then determined primarily by more numerous minor crimes for which indexes are dubious. Weighted indexes reduce but do not eliminate the problem.[13] Thus emphasis must be placed upon certain specific crimes for which indexes are relatively reliable. Fortunately this is possible and in fact enhances our approach to the basic analytical questions of the changes in crime accompanying social modernisation.

An underlying assumption of much theoretical literature on crime is that it is the fact of non-conformity which is fundamental and that delinquency therefore can be treated as a unity. Differences between the aims and causes of, and even participants in, various types of crimes are frequently glossed over in favour of an explanation which simply describes why people choose to act in ways which society defines as delinquent, regardless of the nature of their acts. An important assumption of the present study, for which evidence is presented in the following chapters, is that such an approach is unrealistic. Delinquency cannot be treated as a monolith; no single explanation for all delinquent behaviour is possible unless it is done in such general terms as to be useless. Here, then, is another reason for focusing upon specific crime categories as opposed to a general crime index.

Even the best crime indexes retain certain built-in distortions, some of which operate randomly while others operate systematically. Several problems are particularly germane. International comparisons of crime rates, even for 'good' indexes such as homicide, are exceedingly hazardous due to variations in definitions of crime as well as in report, arrest and trial policies. Comparisons between areas within a given legal system or comparisons of rates in one area through time are more reliable, but even here variations in police efficiency and policy must be noted. And this points to a second problem. For several reasons, the dark figure in the nineteenth century appears to have contained an urban-rural differential which affected patterns of crime both longitudinally and cross-sectionally, i.e. through both time and space. What is known about early nineteenth-century village life and traditions suggests that minor violence and malicious mischief may have been looked upon more lightly in the countryside than in the city. The social order is less fragile in small, stable communities; minor violence or pranks may have served as a traditional outlet for village tensions, and victim, offender and law-enforcement officials were likely to have been acquainted, causing crimes to be settled informally. Crimes of violence, therefore, may have gone unrecorded more often in rural areas and in the early nineteenth century than in more modern, urban settings; rural gendarme reports in Württemberg in fact included no category of assault and battery until 1890.[14] On the contrary, however, village traditions protecting property as well as the relative infrequency of property crimes in the countryside (documented later) may have caused property crimes to be considered more serious and to receive more attention by both police and public in rural areas. Thus rural rates of property crimes appear inflated relative to urban, while rates of rural violence are underestimated relative to urban. Moreover, the distortion operated through time as well; as society became increasingly urbanised, the visibility of property crimes seems to have decreased (which may explain the distortion in court records noted earlier) while the visibility of violence increased. And it should be stressed that, while this bias exists in all records, it was reinforced at each stage of the judicial process and thus is more serious in court than in police records.

Finally, we must keep in mind that we will be examining primarily lower-class crime. Over and over again it has been demonstrated that the selection process which determines what crimes will be reported, who will be arrested, and who will be tried is subject to class biases. The well-to-do are tried relatively infrequently for the crimes they commit; the fact that the majority of persons who turn up in courts and in prisons are poor and/or members of minority groups tells us almost nothing about what kinds of persons commit crimes. Regardless of what crime indexes we use, therefore, but especially when we rely on court records, we will be studying lower-class crime for two reasons. First, we have eliminated class-specific 'white-collar' crimes such as embezzlement because of the unreliability of their indexes. And

secondly, although the types of crimes chosen for examination are by
no means uniquely lower-class crimes, it is members of the lower classes
which largely turn up in these figures.

With these considerations in mind, the following discussion focuses
primarily upon a few key crime categories such as homicide, assault and
battery, and theft. Other categories of crime are examined briefly, but,
given the preceding considerations, the results cannot be taken as
seriously. The analysis is based upon three basic sets of data. Court
records in France and Germany allow cross-sectional comparisons of
crime rates in the 86 departments of France and the 83 *Regierungs-
Bezirke* of Germany at specific points around the end of the century.
Courts records also must be relied upon for an estimate of the behaviour
of national crime rates through time in Germany, but statistics of persons tried have been used in place of the more frequently cited index
of convictions. These do not begin until 1882; no national index is
possible for Germany prior to unification, and for this early period we
must rely upon court and police records from several large states such
as Bavaria and Prussia to provide an estimate of trends. Somewhat
better national time-series indexes are available for France: annual
reports of the Ministry of Justice between 1831 and 1910 included
statistics of cases dropped by public prosecutors and by combining
these with cases tried, an index which approximates crimes known to
public prosecutors is possible.[15] Since a high percentage of crimes
known to the police was supposed to have reached the prosecutor's
office, this new index is clearly an improvement over court records.
Finally, in addition to the cross-sectional and longitudinal analyses
of national data, a number of areas have been selected from both
Germany and France for closer examination. Due to the absence of
good, local police statistics in France, the areas selected here had to
be departments and the crime indexes court records. In Germany,
however, police statistics have been found for a number of urban as
well as rural areas. These statistics provide detailed information about
the movement of crime rates through time in a variety of areas and thus
allow a perspective absent from the cross-sectional analysis.

All historical sources — and especially statistical sources — have
certain problems and pitfalls. Even a date of birth or the contents or a
speech cannot always be accepted as given, and the problems faced by
those who have the courage to delve into past mortality rates or wage
levels are complex indeed. Historical crime records are no different in
this respect; they are neither more nor less problematic than many
types of historical documents and, as is often the case, they provide one

of the few available sources of information for what is a vital historical phenomenon. And if we are careful what we ask of crime statistics; if we keep in mind some of the more obvious distortions, then we can have some confidence that what we will see will reflect reality.

The Theory: Making Sense of the Data

Once the basic contours of nineteenth-century criminal behaviour have been drawn in, we will be faced inevitably with the problem of interpretation. Understanding crime, as the experiences of the past years have made abundantly clear, is no simple undertaking. A voluminous and often contradictory body of criminological explanations exists, even within scholarly literature: delinquent behaviour can be viewed as a personality defect, as mental illness, as learned behaviour, as a culturally motivated and transmitted phenomenon, as a breakdown of social constraints, as a manifestation of social disorganisation or of anomie. Indeed, this wide diversity of interpretations may be yet another reason why historians have been reluctant to tackle the crime phenomenon. This is not the place to survey the whole literature, some of which proves irrelevant. Rather, we will concentrate here upon three specific orientations, two of which have not received enough and one of which has received too much attention in the literature on crime.

The explanation which attributes crime to social disorganisation has proved extremely popular because it is intuitively so persuasive; although no longer so overwhelmingly popular among theorists as it was once, many of its assumptions still underlie much thinking about both crime and the city. Because it is so directly relevant to the questions of urbanisation and social change which concern us here, it is worth discussing in some detail.

Empirically, this explanation of delinquency had its roots in the 'ecological' school of urban studies which grew up around Robert E. Parks at the University of Chicago during the nineteen-twenties and 'thirties. Using mapping techniques, researchers such as Clifford Shaw and his associate Henry McKay found that certain sections of the city were characterised by physical deterioration, poverty, the lack of facilities for maintaining community organisations and high residential mobility. These characteristics suggested a breakdown of social organisation in these areas. The fact that such 'disorganised' sections of the city also tended to have high rates of drunkenness, prostitution and crime indicated that delinquency was associated with, and perhaps an index of, social disorganisation.[16]

The concept of social disorganisation is closely related to the concept of anomie, which has provided an extremely popular explanation for crime as well as suicide.[17] Social disorganisation refers to the disruption or disappearance of social systems; anomie, in the sense in which it is commonly understood, means normlessness and refers to a disruption or disappearance of value systems. The two terms thus refer to similar situations taking place in different spheres. In fact, societal or institutional dislocations are frequently considered a primary cause of anomie since value systems often reflect or are bound up with social systems, and a change in one sphere may be reflected in the other. The two concepts, therefore, are closely interrelated.

Superficially at least, a link between crime, normlessness and social disorganisation seems reasonable. Crime is a form of disorder since it suggests a breakdown of the public consensus or morality; the concept and definition of crime, after all, are products of a system of belief.[18] What is more logical than to seek its roots in a general societal and moral disorder? And if the observer feels that the city represents a kind of disorder, a disruption of traditional values and community organisation, the connection between crime and the city is clear.

This explanation meshes well with a concept of urbanism which received widespread acceptance during the early twentieth century and is still influential today.[19] In this theory, which is built largely upon a deductive base, urbanism is an independent variable which produces a distinct and universal mentality, behaviour, and social organisation. There is such a thing as 'urban man' and 'urban life' and, by implication, also such an entity as a distinctly rural man and rural life. Rural and urban are assumed to be opposite poles on a continuum and urbanisation represents an historical — and traumatic — movement between these two poles.

The essential ingredients for this urban concept were provided by a number of nineteenth-century theorists such as Henry Maine, Ferdinand Tönnies, William Graham Sumner, Emile Durkheim and Max Weber who suggested that urban life is characterised by formal, rationalised, enacted social organisations which place great responsibility upon the individual. Traditional rural life, on the other hand, is dominated by spontaneous, informal social organisations founded upon tradition and kinship and characterised by collective responsibility.

By an accumulation of such ideas, later brought together and systematised by Georg Simmel and Louis Wirth, a concept of urbanism emerged which stresses the atomisation, the individualism, the personal stresses and anxieties, the prevalence of secondary relationships and specialised roles, and the secularism of the urban way of life.[20] Rural

characteristics are assumed to be the opposite of urban and, since the
nature of urban man and urban life is so radically different from that
of rural man and life, it is only natural to assume that urbanisation
must be accompanied by substantial personal and social disorganisation.
Moreover, since urban life means a reduction in collective restraints and
an increase in individual responsibility, it is assumed that more people
would turn to crime in the anonymity of the city than in a more
personal rural setting.

This concept of the city and the link between crime and social disorganisation which it implies have proved extremely resilient, surfacing
again recently in some accounts of the modernisation process.[21] The
model has been seriously criticised, however.[22] In the first place, the
assumption that urban areas or at least lower-class urban areas and
ghettoes lack social organisation and established value systems has been
shown to be naive. Such areas may not be characterised by the types of
values and organisations to which middle-class observers are accustomed
or which they usually are even allowed to see, but alternate forms of
social organisations certainly do exist, even in urban areas of high
mobility. High rates of delinquency could presumably still be attributed
to the shock of transition from one type of organisation to another or
to delinquent value and social systems, but they cannot be attributed to
an absence of social organisation.

A second criticism is that the urban theorists greatly exaggerated the
contrasts between urban and rural life and therefore also the disruption
caused by urbanisation. It has been pointed out in recent years that the
idea of a rural-urban continuum is misleading. Many of the characteristics attributed to rural life are not to be found in actual rural or folk
communities. The communalism and harmony of folk society are often
much less pervasive than commonly assumed; impersonality and anonymity may occur in small isolated communities as well as in large cities,
while at the same time urbanites can and often do have very close interpersonal relationships, including close contact with kin. The stability
of the little community and the attribution of instability to urbanisation have not been upheld by recent investigations. On the contrary,
there are many disruptive aspects in rural social life; distrust, suspicion
and social tension, for example, characterise many folk communities.

Rural communities may thus be more 'urban' than is commonly
supposed. But, on the other hand, urban communities can be more
'rural' than the idea of a rural-urban continuum suggests. Urban
theorists such as Simmel and Wirth deduced many of their 'urban'
characteristics from demographic factors. The fact of a large, dense

population, for example, was assumed to imply interaction with large numbers of people which in turn resulted in the predominance of impersonal, secondary relationships, high degrees of personal anxiety, the rejection of traditional communal values and structures in favour of more individualised ones, and so on. But Durkheim himself had pointed out that potential interaction does not necessarily mean actual interaction; in his terms, 'physical density' may increase without a corresponding increase in 'moral density' because an increase in the density of a population may take place by an accretion of relatively isolated cells or segments. Although it has often been assumed that this form of urban growth broke down with the industrial revolution and the rise of large, industrial cities, more recent studies such as those of Herbert Gans and Oscar Lewis have found that this phenomenon still occurs.[23] Pockets of traditional society remain in large cities and often their isolation and 'rural' social characteristics increase under the impact of urban life. In fact, traditional values and patterns of behaviour may be, and often are, retained within the urban context even though the population may not be separated into clearly isolated units.

The fact that the disruption of social life with urbanisation has been overemphasised suggests that the personal disruption created by joining the ranks of city dwellers may be less than is commonly supposed. That differences between urban and rural life are not so great as is sometimes presumed, that some traditional values, patterns of behaviour and organisations are maintained in the city which can serve as familiar landmarks for the newcomer, that the newcomer often may, if he so desires, even move directly into a small replica of his home community which persists within the city — all this warns against overstatement of the traditional urbanist view.

Thus, while situations of social disorganisation and anomie may well result in delinquent behaviour, urbanisation does not necessarily lead to disorganisation and anomie; urbanisation, in other words, is probably not the great dissolver of morality and society which it has been assumed to be. The transition from a rural to an urban way of life undoubtedly involves adjustments, and delinquency may conceivably be connected with the transition. But it is doubtful whether the concepts of anomie and disorganisation can provide an adequate explanation for such a connection.

The preceding account of the anomie theory is of course greatly simplified; since Durkheim's day, the concept of anomie has been developed in a wide range of subtle and complex theories often bearing little resemblance to the original concept. Moreover, urbanisation is by

no means the only process which theorists have felt could give rise to a
situation of anomie and thus to delinquency. Another was suggested by
Robert K. Merton in a suggestive and influential article entitled 'Social
Structure and Anomie', originally published in 1938, and this provides
our second and more subtle theory to be tested.[24] According to Merton,
anomie and therefore delinquency result from a discrepancy between
the goals which a society sets for its members and the means which it
legitimises for attaining them. Any society provides certain culturally
defined goals for its members – in modern Western cultures these
include material wealth and high social status – as well as norms
defining which means are considered acceptable for the attainment of
these goals. Thrift and social mobility, for instance, are considered legitimate means of attaining wealth; theft and violence are not. Anomie
and, therefore, delinquency (although delinquency is not the only
possible result of such anomie according to Merton) may occur when
society's goals have been internalised but its norms governing means
have not – as would be the case if great stress were placed upon goals
relative to means or, presumably, if goals were successfully emphasised
by a society while legitimate, socially structured means for attaining
these goals with reasonable effort were lacking. Goals and means would
be out of step if a society succeeded – as the West has done during the
past century or so – in selling certain common material and egalitarian
values to the population at large while its social structure was too rigid
and economic opportunities too few or unequally distributed to allow
access to these values and symbols by all members of society. In such a
situation, some members of society either would reject society's norms
or would become frustrated and turn to crime as a means of reaching
the goals which they share with society at large. As Merton pointed out,
therefore, it is not simply the fact of poverty, nor even of poverty in
the midst of plenty, which results in criminal behaviour; it is unobtain-
able goals and thwarted expectations which lead to delinquency. This
could, we can add, occur in a rural as in an urban context.

  The concept of frustrated goals and expectations sound extremely
familiar in the 1970s, in part because of the idea of a 'revolution of
rising expectations' has gained widespread acceptance, even among the
sociologically unsophisticated, but also because concepts and terms
very similar to those used by Merton are receiving a great deal of attention today in connection with explanations of collective violence.
Theorists such as Ted R. Gurr and James C. Davies have worked out a
theory of collective violence which, since it employs many of the same

concepts as Merton, must be considered as an explanation for delinquent behaviour in general.[25] In fact, it can be argued that the relative deprivation theory developed by Gurr and others to explain revolution is basically a refinement and application of Merton's original ideas, assuming his concepts of goals and frustrated expectations but placing less emphasis on the problem of available means for obtaining them.

Basically, this theory assumes that all men, even in the best of times, are faced with a discrepancy between what they expect or feel they deserve and what they actually obtain. Some gap between expectations and attainment is tolerable but a crisis point is reached when the gap widens rapidly. Various factors may cause the gap to widen. A change in government or rapid industrial development may cause expectations to rise markedly relative to actual conditions; or conditions may worsen rapidly while expectations retain their previous levels, as would be the case in an economic recession. The most volatile situation arises from a pattern that Davies has termed the 'J-curve'. After a period in which both expectations and fulfilment have been rising rapidly at almost the same rate, something happens which causes attainment to fall off rapidly. Expectations, however, continue to rise temporarily and a huge gap suddenly occurs between expectations and attainment. But in any of these situations where there is a widening gap between what people have and what they expect, frustration results. As psychologists have frequently pointed out, frustration often results in aggression.[26] It is, then, when men feel themselves deprived relative to what they have experienced in the past and/or have been led to expect from the future that they rebel.

Relative deprivation theory as developed by Gurr is intended as a social-psychological explanation for collective violence.[27] However, this theory has obvious relevance to the problem of crime as well. The general concept of relative deprivation has often been used to explain the so-called economic crimes, i.e. crimes such as theft and embezzlement which are often considered, perhaps incorrectly, to have basically economic motivations as well as obvious economic expressions. Certainly this is an advance over older explanations which attributed such crimes simply to poverty and want. Gurr has worked out models and specific details of the argument which make this explanation more applicable than previously. To the concept of relative deprivation, however, Gurr's argument adds the frustration-aggression hypothesis, i.e. the idea that frustration often results in overt hostility and aggression on the part of individuals. When this is amplified to include the idea of substitute objects of aggression, the theory logically would seem to have

great potential as an explanation for interpersonal as well as collective
or political violence. As Lewis Coser has pointed out, aggression may be
directed against the original object of hostility, but hostility may also
be deflected against substitute objects which have nothing to do with
the original cause of frustration and hostility.[28] Persons who are frustrated by lack of opportunity and poor living conditions direct their
aggression against government and business only rarely; much more
often these tensions and hostilities are taken out upon members of their
families and neighbourhoods or even in activities such as anti-semitism.
Instead of directing their wrath against the white and somewhat amor-
phous power structure which is responsible for their frustration, for
instance, blacks have often taken out their hostilities upon members of
their own communities — and this is even true of many urban riots.
Relative deprivation which results in frustration, therefore, might lead
to theft and related crimes as a means of obtaining culturally defined
goals of material wealth and social status or even to defy accepted
norms about how such goals are to be achieved; or hostilities arising out
of such frustration could result in interpersonal violence. For in fact it
is only in very unusual circumstances that deprivation is great enough
and frustration pervasive enough to motivate large masses of persons to
direct their aggressions against the state.

Quite possibly, this hypothesis suggests, crime can serve as a safety
valve for society by allowing the release of hostilities and the lessening
of frustration before they can accumulate and become directed against
the foundations of society or against the state.[29] Crime, in other words,
may be an index of frustration and tension in a society, and may be
related in some way to collective violence — either directly as would be
the case if both collective violence and criminal violence were to rise
together in times of severe deprivation or inversely if crime served to
siphon off hostilities that otherwise would be channelled into collective
violence.

Potentially, the applications of this explanation are many. Expectations and relative deprivation, with the incorporation of other concepts
such as the cultural transmission and learning of deviant behaviour,
might be used to explain gross patterns of crime through time and space
as well as deviant behaviour among specific social groups; the concepts
are relevant, for instance, to possible economic correlates of crime but
can also be used to explain the incidence of crime among women or
various ethnic groups. Clearly, then, the theory is worth considering.

A number of criticisms have been directed against the Gurr argument.
As a general explanation of delinquent behaviour, however, only three

basic problems need be anticipated. First, as is the case for many general explanations of criminality, this theory as it presently stands would be forced to account for very different types of crimes with the same arguments. Unless, for example, an added ingredient can be found to explain differences in timing between personal and property crimes, relative deprivation theory would be forced to account for two different phenomena which often appear to fluctuate independently of one another.

Second, differences in expectations and attainments still do not adequately explain why some persons turn to crime and others do not. Relative deprivation theory suggests one possible 'push' factor driving men to criminality by indicating that it is deprivation relative to expectations which leads to frustration, which in turn leads to delinquency. But what is it that determines how this frustration, this 'push' toward crime, will be worked out? It is impossible to believe that degrees of frustration, determined simply by the extent of deprivation, would be a sufficient explanation. Surely cultural milieu, types of social contacts, degree of internalisation of prevailing norms, the availability of legitimate opportunities, the degree to which crime is deterred or 'contained', and so on would have to be taken into account?

And third, while the argument that deprivation leads to frustration which leads to aggression seems convincing and is rooted in solid psychological research, a marvellous number of other causes of frustration could be listed which presumably also should be added to the causes of crime: sexual frustration, frustrations arising out of family situations, frustrations arising out of work or city life which have little to do with deprivation — all would have to be included among the causes of aggression unless some compelling reason can be found to explain why frustrations arising out of deprivation should have particular potency. Thus relative deprivation may be a very limited explanation for criminal violence and also could be very difficult to test.

The criticism that deprivation may be only one of many causes leading to aggression suggests that the problem of crime might usefully be viewed within the larger context of social conflict. As Lewis Coser has pointed out, social conflict is a fundamental and even functional fact of all social life; conflict is an integral aspect of society and not, as many social scientists have assumed, simply a sign of disequilibrium and dysfunction in the system.[30] Conflict arises from hostilities which have many roots: family and community tensions, inequalities in the distribution of wealth and power, social change, the lack of social change — all can and do result in conflict situations. Such hostilities may be expressed in several ways, not all of which appear on the surface to be related to the actual cause of hostility:[31]

1. Hostility can be expressed as what Coser terms 'realistic' conflict, i.e. directed expressly at the actual cause of the hostility as, for example, when workers disturbed over wages go on strike for higher pay. (But note too that hostilities in one area of life may serve to reinforce hostilities and conflicts elsewhere; the willingness to strike, for example, may be heightened by tensions and conflicts at home.)
2. Hostility may also be expressed as 'non-realistic' conflict when tensions are relieved by taking hostilities out upon a substitute object as in the case of much anti-Semitism and many racial conflicts. Tensions arising out of a work situation or even basic changes in the structure of the economy and society, for instance, may be expressed as conflict within the family.
3. Tensions may be relieved by activity short of actual conflict.

The first two of these possibilities suggest that criminal behaviour might reasonably be viewed as a form of social conflict. This is most easily seen with regard to such types of crime as criminal violence or even arson which obviously involve conflict and can be assumed, without a great deal of imagination, to arise often from various sorts of tensions in the family and in society. Some violence, for instance, is aimed directly at the cause of hostility: rural workers sometimes burn the buildings of landlords who offend them and wives kill husbands, again often because of tensions arising directly out of their relationship. But much of such crime might also be seen as an expression of tensions arising elsewhere which need release. Clearly, therefore, it should be possible to interpret at least some violent crime as a form of social conflict.

But what of a crime such as theft? Can it be seen as a form of conflict? Perhaps such crimes do serve in some way as a form of 'non-realistic' conflict, a release from tensions and frustrations which has little to do with the real cause of hostility.[32] In the context of relative deprivation theory, some theft may even be seen as a form of realistic conflict since it is aimed more or less directly at reaching certain goals. In fact, the following statements from persons in two very different situations, both of whom were considered delinquent by their societies, suggest that property crimes such as theft consciously may serve as such forms of realistic conflict. Joseph Kürper, a vagrant who turned

thief and swindler in nineteenth-century Germany, at least in retro-
spect saw his crimes in this way:

> At first I bore no ill-will to the well-to-do, and I had no quarrel with
> those who had treated me so harshly. Gradually, however, I realised
> my grievance against society and began to wage war on it by acts of
> pilfering, the first of which I committed in the house of a small
> farmer where my mother was in service. Tormented by hunger, I
> got in through a window and stole a loaf of bread and a few
> kreutzers. This was my first theft and it had bad results for me, for,
> when taxed with it, I confessed and was cruelly flogged by the
> farmer. Out of revenge I killed one of his fowls every day.[33]

And this rationale is even more explicit in Eldridge Cleaver's *Post-
Prison Writings and Speeches*, published a century later in 1969:

> Can one person engage in civil war? . . . I would say that one person
> acting alone could in fact be engaged in a civil war against an oppres-
> sive system. That's how I look upon those cats in those penitenti-
> aries. I don't care what they're in for — robbery, burglary, rape,
> murder, kidnap, anything. A response to a situation. A response to
> an environment. Any social science book will tell you that if you
> subject people to an unpleasant environment, you can predict that
> they will rebel against it . . .[34]

Both of these witnesses interpreted criminal offences as forms of protest, a kind of rebellion against an unjust society. Both viewed their
acts as social conflict aimed directly or indirectly at the cause of their
frustrations. Thus it might be useful to interpret at least some crimes
as just one among many forms of social conflict rather than as irrational,
dysfunctional, pathological behaviour.

Each of these three explanations which will be tested or used in this
study — the social disorganisation, the relative deprivation, and the
social conflict models — involve the question of causation. Indeed,
problems of causation are inevitable in any serious analysis of crime;
almost all studies of crime attempt, in some manner, to explain why
crime occurs or why crime rates vary. As the preceding discussion
has indicated, the present investigation is no different in this respect for
it too must grapple with problems of explanation. However, for several
reasons a coherent theoretical explanation of crime is not of ultimate
concern here. First, this is primarily a work of history, not sociology;

focus is upon particular, historical patterns of crime in relation to the industrialisation process, not upon the crime phenomenon in general. More important, this study represents an attempt, however tentative, to shift focus away from explaining crime to interpreting crime, that is, to shift attention away from an exclusive focus upon what causes crime to a deeper appreciation of the significance or social meaning of crime. What function, if any, does crime play for the individual and what does it mean to the individual who participates in it? What function might it play for society? For if criminal behaviour is related to other historical developments and in addition actually fulfils a function for the offender or for society, it can reveal a great deal not only about a particular society but also about social processes. In other words, we need to get away from exclusive forms of explanation that leave no time dimension, no adjustment for social processes. Perhaps criminal activity in a period of social change, reflects particular tensions and dislocations; perhaps in such circumstances delinquent behaviour can serve as an outlet for pent-up frustrations, even as a means of protesting against trends in society or against prevailing social norms. Or conversely, perhaps criminal activity for many offenders represents an attempt to adapt, although in ways which society regards as illegitimate, to prevailing social goals. If so, changes in delinquent behaviour, when they occur, may reflect changes in value or institutional systems. Perhaps criminal behaviour can become an outlet for emotions and needs which can also be expressed through other channels including such 'legitimate' activities as trade unionism, social advancement, and so on. In terms of existing theory, this could mean that one concept best fits one stage of industrialisation, and another a later stage. This is the historical dimension missing from theory to date.

Viewed from this vantage point, which represents a slightly different way of looking at a familiar phenomenon from that usually adopted in theoretical treatments of criminal causation, crime may be of wider interest than is commonly assumed. If crime does serve some function, if it is closely related to other social, economic or even political processes, and if it is participated in by large numbers of people, then it cannot be dismissed as an isolated phenomenon confined to the dregs of society. Crime may tell something about society itself and what is happening to it, and therefore may be an important key which is often overlooked.[35] Durkheim's suggestion of a relationship between anomie and suicide was important not only because it provided a new explanation for suicide, but also because it caused a reorientation in approaches to suicide. Seen as a reflection of anomie, suicide could be considered as a window to society and its values. Similarly, by seeking to interpret as well as explain crime, a wider significance may be discovered for it than is usually recognised. Certainly its sheer mass as well as its persistence compel historical attention.

2 PATTERNS OF PROPERTY CRIME

Whether they are fearful citizens discussing the threat of crime or academicians investigating some aspect of delinquency, most people distinguish between crimes against property and crimes of violence against persons. Such a distinction has merit, of course, and we will honour that division here. Nevertheless, several qualifications to this approach do need to be noted. Unfortunately the division is not quite so neat as it first appears. The category 'property crimes', for example, includes a number of crimes such as malicious mischief and arson which, although they do involve property, are in motivation and nature similar to crimes of violence. And this again raises questions about the feasibility of any general index of property crimes: is it possible to say anything meaningful about property crime in general? The case of arson illustrates one objection: a general index of property crimes would include many crimes which in fact have little in common and thus would obscure important differences. But secondly, the accuracy of indexes for these various crimes varies greatly. Frequently committed minor crimes such as 'rural offences', malicious mischief or thefts of firewood would be fascinating to study, but their indexes are extremely unreliable. Arson, a more serious and rather rare offence, would also be interesting to investigate as a form of violence against property, but again indexes are poor. The same can be said for fraud and embezzlement. Thus while we will note patterns of some other crimes briefly, primary emphasis must be limited to theft as a crime of importance for which indexes are sufficiently reliable to warrant investigation.[1]

We will begin with the most obvious questions, which concern rates and trends on a national basis. Were rates higher in Germany than in France during the nineteenth century? Did property crime rates rise or fall during the course of the century? The answers, if not always definitive, have serious implications. Apparent variations in national crime rates can be — and have been — attributed to differences in national character or culture, to differences in levels of modernisation, or to national differences in moral standards. Similarly, trends in rates may be used to buttress a wide range of theories and prejudices. A perceived increase in theft rates can be related to a decline in moral standards and respect for property, to changes in child rearing practices or family patterns, to the waning influence of religion, to decreasing police effectiveness, to 'easy' courts, to rising greed, or to the corrosive nature of modern, urban life. What starts out as a set of purely factual problems clearly becomes both politically and academically important. Whether the problems can be resolved — or if resolved, have any meaning on a national basis is less obvious. Nevertheless, since we are accustomed to thinking in national terms and since national data are available for both Germany and France during the nineteenth century, national averages provide a useful starting-point. The first task, in other words, is a descriptive survey of the behaviour of national property crime rates through time, and this occupies the first two sections of this chapter.

One of the oldest and most common sense explanations for the behaviour of theft rates through time is that which stresses the importance of material conditions.[2] That theft, a crime which involves the taking of economic goods, should be related to economic conditions in general is logical, of course. But the explanation is not as clear-cut as it at first sounds. Some commentators have stressed need; people steal, according to this hypothesis, because of material hardship and want. Others have emphasised greed; people steal not because they need something but because they simply want something which they cannot afford or are too lazy to work for. Recent explanations are more sophisticated and sometimes incorporate both positions; relative deprivation theory, for example, would imply that man's assessment of need is relative rather than absolute. But the connection is not at all well defined and is far from being universally recognised.

While economic conditions can and have been used to explain both trends and levels of theft, the greatest appeal of this explanation has been in connection with yearly or seasonal fluctuations in theft rates. A wide range of possible explanations for a long-range trend in rates can be imagined, but causation for the constant dips and rises in theft rates seems less obvious. To be sure, specific peaks and troughs might be explained on an *ad hoc* basis; a war, a revolution, a bad winter might explain certain unusual years. But fluctuating economic conditions are the most obvious explanation for constant oscillations in theft rates.

However, while the topic has received a great deal of attention, it is not yet clear what actual correlation can be seen between changes in economic conditions and in thefts. A few students have claimed to find a positive correlation between material well-being and theft. In a report to the Magistry of Lancashire in 1824 and again in a paper read before the British Association for the Advancement of Science in 1854, the Rev. John Clay maintained that:

It has long been a popular opinion that committals to prison increase
under the pressure of 'bad times', and diminish when that pressure is
removed. This opinion appears to be in many respects erroneous . . .
'bad times' may add a few cases to the sessions calendars, and . . .
'good times' greatly aggravate summary convictions; . . . the increase
to the sessions consists of the young and thoughtless who, when
thrown into idleness, are liable to lapse into dishonesty; and . . . the
increase of summary cases arises from the intemperance which high
wages encourage among the ignorant and sensual.

He concluded, therefore, that 'want and distress, uncombined with dis-
solute habits are rarely operative in producing crime', and that 'high
wages to the ignorant and uneducated poor, bring with them the means
of gratifying the propensity to intoxication, which is so fatal to their
comfort and character'.[3]

This conclusion, though popular among the middle classes during the
nineteenth century, generally has not been borne out by more careful
observations. One of the earliest truly statistical studies of crime, an
analysis of Bavarian police records by Georg von Mayr in 1867, claimed
to find a strong positive connection between theft and hardship.[4] In
1929, W. Woytinsky applied modern correlational techniques to this
same data and obtained a rather high correlation of $r=0.76$ between
theft and grain prices.[5] Similarly a number of other analysts have
claimed to find a positive connection between theft and material hardship in Europe during the nineteenth century.

These results have not gone undisputed and a few students have
claimed to find no significant correlation between the two phenomena.
A number of reasons for disagreement can be cited. The crime indexes
as well as the economic indicators which were used have varied. A wide
array of methods of analysis have been used. Areas and time-periods
investigated have not always been the same. For various reasons the
issue has been controversial, therefore, and this is one justification for
the rather lengthy examination of the problem in the third section of
this chapter.

The fourth section examines possible correlations between theft
rates, city size and urban growth. Community size is a common explanation for the theft rates: theft rates are usually assumed to be higher in
cities than in the countryside. Explanations vary: theft is easier to
commit and get away with in large cities; less respect for private property is to be found in cities; urban growth is thought to be accompanied by social disorganisation and/or moral decay which results in the

breakdown of law and order and so on. But did a correlation actually
obtain between community size and crime in the nineteenth century?
If so, was this simply due to the nature of urban life or was it the disruption caused by first learning to live in the city, i.e was it the fact of
urban life of the process of urban growth? Finally, is this an adequate
explanation for trends in national rates and for differences in international and intranational levels of theft?

Overall, in all four sections, the focus is on two problems: the effect
of material conditions and of urbanism upon theft rates. But the first
task is primarily descriptive; national patterns must be outlined and
possible correlates of theft rates suggested. Only after correlations have
been established can alternative explanations be weighed, which is our
final purpose.

National Patterns: Levels and Long-Term Trends

Trial statistics suggest significant differences in the incidence of property crimes in Germany and France at the turn of the century.
Average rates of persons tried 1900-9 were much higher in Germany
than in France for all three categories of crimes listed in Table 2.1.[6]
Two-and-a-half times as many persons were tried for theft per 100,000
adults in Germany as in France during that period. French arson rates
were one-third and fraud-embezzlement rates less than one-fifth those
in Germany. Apparent differences in levels of property crimes, then, are
consistent and substantial.

Table 2.1: Average Rates of Property Crimes per 100,000 Adults in
Germany and France, 1900-9

	Germany Persons tried	France Persons tried	Cases reported
Theft group	334.34	135.02	392.80
Fraud-embezzlement	153.87	25.60	73.43
Arson	1.57	0.52	6.31

To what extent these figures reflect actual differences in the incidence of property crimes is difficult to say with any precision; the
effect of variables such as definitions of crime as well as recording,
detection and prosecution efficiency and practices cannot be quanti-
fied. However, there is reason to believe that actual differences were
much less than these statistics suggest. German prosecutors appear to

have been under greater pressure to bring cases to trial than were their
French counterparts.[7] German courts, consequently, probably received
a higher percentage of known cases than did the French. When this
factor is discounted, estimates at least of theft rates are more similar,
though some difference remains. Rates of persons tried for theft in
Germany, although considerably higher than similar statistics for
France, were slightly less than French rates of cases known to public
prosecutors. This in itself, of course, proves little since not all cases
known to prosecutors came to trial in Germany as well as France and
because one index is based on numbers of persons and the other on
numbers of cases. However, if it is estimated that statistics of cases
reported in France represent only about 70 per cent of the persons
associated with them and that only about 60 per cent of all cases of
theft in France were solved — estimates based on somewhat meagre
information but intended to err in a direction that will overstate French
rates — an estimate of persons who would be tried in France if all cases
except those which were unsolved came to court is still less than the
German rate.[8] This is of course a very gross estimate. Nevertheless, it
can be suggested that, while the differences between theft rates in the
two countries were not as large as a superficial comparison would
suggest, French theft rates probably were slightly lower than German.

While perhaps not in keeping with national stereotypes (e.g. the
obedient, law-abiding German), this would of course be consistent with
the contention that theft is associated with urbanisation and modern
life since German society by 1900 was considerably more urban and
industrial than the French.[9] Again, though, the tenuous nature of this
estimate must be emphasised. Moreover, it would be foolhardy to
attempt even such gross estimates for the fraud-embezzlement group
and for arson due to the extreme unreliability of these indexes and, in
the case of arson, the small numbers involved.

Comparisons of long-term trends in property crime may be made
with a bit more confidence than comparisons of crime levels, though
even such estimates are plagued with problems. The most accessible
index of total property crimes in France, statistics of persons tried in
assize courts, fell 72 per cent between the early 1830s and the end of
the first decade in the twentieth century, but this drop reflects an
increasing tendency to try property crimes in lower courts. Table 2.2
presents average rates of both cases reported and persons tried for
several property crimes for each decade from the 1830s through the
first decade of the present century. Where appropriate, statistics from
both correctional and assize courts have been combined. These indexes

provide a quite different picture. Significant increases between the
1830s and the early 1900s are apparent in all indexes except arson even
when trial statistics are used, but using rates of cases reported the
increase becomes massive. The fraud-embezzlement group, for instance,
rose over 600 per cent during the period. Theft rates in the 1900s were
230 per cent above those in the 1830s. Only arson rates remained relatively steady though they rose slightly. Moreover, this pattern of rising
rates persists even if the 1840s, a period of extraordinarily high property
crime rates, is used rather than the 1830s as a point of comparison.

Table 2.2: Rates of Property Crimes in France, 1830-1910, Averaged by
Decade

	Crimes reported (r) and crimes tried (t)					
	Theft		Fraud-embezzlement		Arson	
	r	t	r	t	r	t
1830s[a]	119.03	84.16	9.94	7.79	5.44	0.56
1840s	167.38	114.60	17.33	12.75	7.24	0.89
1850s	236.55	150.20	23.43	19.58	8.80	1.02
1860s	234.42	132.09	35.93	23.50	6.29	0.82
1870s[b]	283.72	145.08	39.89	23.77	5.62	0.69
1880s	333.98	154.12	52.94	27.64	6.41	0.81
1890s	374.06	154.42	64.48	26.75	6.01	0.74
1900s	392.80	135.02	73.43	25.60	6.31	0.52
Change, 1830s 1900s	+230%	+60%	+639%	+229%	+16%	--7%
Change, 1840s 1900s	+135%	+18%	+324%	+101%	− 13%	−42%

[a]1830 excluded in crimes reported.
[b]excluding 1870-1.

Long-range national trends are difficult to assess for Germany because of the lack of an index comparable to the French index of crimes
made known to prosecutors and because of the absence of national
statistics before 1882. Trial statistics indicate a rise in rates of persons
tried for fraud between the 1880s and the first decade of the twentieth
century, but a decline in both arson and theft (Table 2.3). The decline
in theft, if true, would be highly significant. However, various regional
and local police statistics suggest that this trend may be inaccurate.
During this time Germany becamse more than 50 per cent urban and,
as will be demonstrated later, all cities for which police statistics are
available experienced rising theft rates during this period. In addition,
some evidence is available of rising theft rates even in rural areas. The

Table 2.3: Rates of Persons Tried for Property Crimes in Germany, 1882-1912, Averaged by Decade

	Theft group	Fraud-embezzlement	Arson
1882-89	361.03	108.13	2.46
1890 99	351.99	141.89	2.01
1900-9	334.34	153.87	1.57
1910-12	325.29	168.15	1.22
Change			
1880s-1900s	−7%	+42%	−36%

rate of theft cases reported and followed up by gendarmes in Baden during the same period rose from 306.4 cases per 100,000 of the total population in 1883/85 to 426.4 in 1911/13, a rise of 39.2 per cent.[10] Likewise, the rate of thefts reported to gendarmes in Württemberg rose 78.2 per cent between the years 1890/3 and 1909/12.[11] Thus the trend in theft rates in national court records probably reflects biases caused by a growing population and overworked legal and law enforcement machinery. This is the situation which has been seen for France, where similar factors caused theft rates in court records to be underesti mated; between the 1880s and the 1900s, in fact, French court records show a decline in theft rates while cases reported rose 18 per cent. That such factors were also at work in Germany is suggested by arrest rates for theft in Württemberg, which declined while report rates rose between 1890 and 1912.[12]

National trends prior to the beginning of the national court records are more difficult to estimate. The best statistics available before 1882 are statistics of new judicial investigations in the eight 'old' provinces of Prussia from 1854 to 1878 and statistics of cases reported to the police in the seven districts of Bavaria east of the Rhine from 1835 to 1860 (Tables 2.4 and 2.5).[13] These indexes are not of course directly com- parable to the Reich statistics, but they do provide reasonably reliable crime indexes for several large areas of Germany prior to unification.

In general, the direction of trends in the property crime indexes are consistent with those in the later Reich indexes. Arson rates declined in Prussia as they did later in the Reich, for instance, but again this trend in court records must be treated with suspicion. The Bavarian records, being indexes of cases reported, are probably more reliable; in these records, crimes of damage to property, of which arson accounted for roughly two-thirds in 1850/1, rose 44 per cent during the period. Similarly, arson rates calculated from fire insurance records rose

Table 2.4: Average Rates of New Investigations for Property Crimes in the Eight 'Old' Provinces of Prussia, 1854-78[a]

	Theft group	Fraud-embezzlement	Arson
1854-59	292.97	1.65	40.95
1860-69	236.26	1 64	35.22
1870-78	215.12	1.44	37.39
Change			
1850s 1870s	−27%	−13%	−9%

[a]Per 100,000 civilian inhabitants of all ages.

Table 2 5: Average Rates of Reported Property Crimes in Bavaria East of the Rhine, 1835-60[a]

	Theft group	Damage group
1835-39	269.4	12.9
1840-49	289.7	12.7
1850-59	321.7	18.6
Change		
1830s-1850s	+19%	+44%

[a]Per 100,000 total inhabitants.
[b]This is a broad category in these records and includes embezzlement, poaching, etc.

approximately 122 per cent in Württemberg between 1861/70 and 1891/7.[14]

Theft rates in Prussia, which were surprisingly similar to Reich rates, fell as they did later in the Reich, but statistics of thefts and related crimes rose in Bavaria. Again, this could reflect real differences in crime patterns but the Prussian records are basically court records and may be biased against thefts. Rates of persons arrested for thefts and reported by gendarmes in the rural area of Baden between 1831/39 and 1881/9 rose almost 100 per cent, even when rates are calculated in such a way as to inflate rates from the earlier period.[15]

For both Germany and France, but especially for Germany, the magnitude of the change in property crime rates cannot be determined accurately; the most that can be offered with any degree of certainty is a rather gross estimate of the direction of these long-term trends. And again, the unreliability of the fraud and arson indexes must be emphasised. However, there is little apparent reason to reject outright the broad

trends in thefts suggested by these figures. The German statistics do
come from court records, but rough checks against other data were
possible. In the case of France the figures used, in spite of their
deficiencies, approximate an index of crimes reported to public prosecutors and thus should avoid many of the biases inherent in court
records. Of course, the percentage of crimes actually recorded may have
increased somewhat during the century, but this increase would probably have been mainly concentrated in the early years of the century
when police forces with crime functions were first being developed; it is
unlikely that increased reporting is sufficient to explain the sustained
long-term rise in theft levels. And while some changes in the administration of justice did take place in France during the century, their
relevance to the recording of major crimes such as theft was slight.[16]
These statistics, then, can probably be considered accurate in broad
outline and offer as good a picture of average crime rates in Germany
and France as is likely to be found.

Thus in both Germany and France a general rise in property crimes
seems likely and a rise in theft rates during the nineteenth century
highly probable. This increase of course coincides with substantial
urbanisation and industrialisation in both countries, suggesting a link
between theft and modernisation. However, these results are too inexact
to be more than suggestive; trend estimates are too imprecise, for
instance, to allow the slope of trends in crime to be compared to the
speed of modernisation, and two cases are too few to allow meaningful
comparisons. More precise tests require analysis of criminal behaviour
in smaller areas and, where possible, comparisons of short-term national
trends.

National Trends: Cycles and Short-Term Trends

This pattern of rising theft and fraud rates as well as constant or declining rates of recorded arson is confirmed by semilogarithmic graphs
of cases reported in France, shown in Fig. 2.1.[17] However, several
trends were not linear.[18] Moreover, each index was subject to significant fluctuations, especially during the first half of the period. The
years of crisis and revolution in the late 1840s and the years around
1870 appear to have been crucial periods in two of the indexes; both
theft and arson experienced their most violent fluctuations around
1848 and, relatedly, fluctuations in both indexes became less marked
and trends in theft as well as in fraud-embezzlement altered somewhat
in slope after the founding of the Third Republic. In fact, as the figures
in this and the following chapter will demonstrate, a basic alteration in

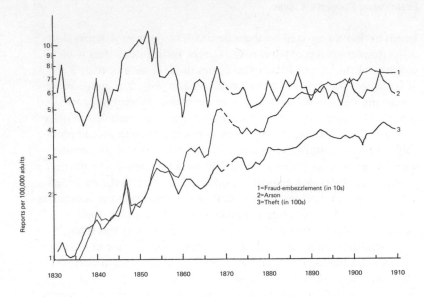

Fig 2.1: Rates of reported property crimes in France, 1831-1910.

Fig 2.2: Rates of persons tried for property crimes in the German Reich, 1882-1912

Fig 2.3: Rates of reported property crimes in Bavaria east of the Rhine, 1835-60

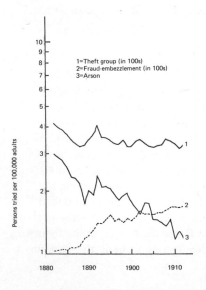

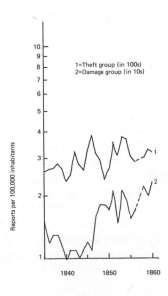

the behaviour of most crime rates seems to have occurred somewhere around the 1860s or 1870s, suggesting that the history of crime in France, at least on the national level, should be divided into two periods with the turning-point occurring around 1870, with a decade of margin in either direction depending on the precise aspect of crime in question.

Theft rates, for instance, rose steadily through the century but the rate of increase was greater before 1870 or perhaps 1880 than after. Deviations from the trend also appear greater before 1870 than after, though this was largely due to two large peaks in the 'forties and 'fifties. The first was a sharp peak lasting only two years; theft rates moved sharply upward in 1846 and reached a high in 1847, after which they dropped to a low trough in the revolutionary year of 1848. After 1848, however, theft rates again began a steep rise which was longer-lived; after climbing steadily for six years, they reached their highest peak of the period in 1854. They remained high for several years thereafter but dropped steadily, bottoming out finally in 1859. The incidence of theft thus was unusually high in 1846-7 and throughout most of the 1850s, but was low during the revolution of 1848.

Clearly then, the turbulent social history of the first half of the nineteenth century was reflected in the behaviour of French property crime rates. Moreover the most rapid climb and greatest fluctuations in two of the indexes, but especially in the theft rates, coincided with the period when urban growth was most rapid and novel; the rate of increase in total urban population in France was greater during the early years than later, and the turning-point appears to have occurred around 1880, when the growth rate for thefts also began to decline.[19] Again, a connection between these phenomena seems reasonable but cannot be proven on the basis of this data alone.

Similar graphs of persons tried in Germany 1882-1912 (Figure 2.2) confirm the overall trends described previously; rates of persons tried for fraud rose consistently while theft and arson fell, although the probable distortions in these trends must be reiterated. Two of the indexes experienced significant drops or troughs in 1888-90 and unusually high peaks in 1892. On the whole, though, the indexes do not seem terribly volatile. No long-term periodisation of German cycles and trends is possible due to the absence of a long-term series; the Bavarian and Prussian records differ too greatly in nature and scope and do not overlap sufficiently in time to be of much use for such purposes. Nevertheless, it is possible to speculate that a dampening of yearly fluctuations similar to that which seems to have occurred in France after 1870 may also have occurred in Germany by the end of the century.[20]

The 1840s, a period of distinctive crime patterns in France, were years of social and political disruption in Germany as well. For comparative purposes, therefore, it would be interesting to examine German statistics for this period. Unfortunately such statistics are limited, even on a local level. The best series available is the Bavarian. Here the movement of crime rates was remarkably similar to the French. The two crime groups shown in Fig. 2.3, damage to property and the theft group, were both quite volatile during the period, although damage to property experienced the largest fluctuations. Two very large cycles are apparent in the index of damage to property. One spans the period 1840-9, with the peak occurring in 1846. Rates, which had been rising previous to 1846, dropped sharply in the following three years. The second large cycle includes the period 1849-57, with another very high peak being reached in 1853. Interestingly, both of these very high peaks coincide with the two highest peaks in theft rates, though cycles of peaks and troughs are more frequent in the theft index. Most significant here is a longish cycle lasting from 1842 to 1849, with the peak occurring in 1846. The early 'fifties were also a period of rising theft rates, though the peak reached in 1853 was less sharp and not so high as that of the 'forties.

The behaviour of property crime rates in Germany thus was not unlike that of French rates during the same period. As in France, the 'forties and 'fifties were a period of unusually high and turbulent property crime rates and, as in France, the real crisis in thefts occurred several years before the political crisis of 1848. Rates during the crisis of 1848 were in fact quite low in both countries. Unlike France, however, Bavaria's greatest crisis in theft appears to have occurred in the 'forties rather than the 'fifties, and damage to property peaked sooner than in France, where indexes of arson and other destruction of property crested during the revolutionary years.

Bavarian statistics, of course, are not necessarily representative of Germany as a whole. However, the limited statistics available for other areas suggest a similar pattern. Records of arrest for thefts by gendarmes in Württemberg show a significant peak in theft rates in 1846, with a drop the following year.[21] Unfortunately there is a gap in the index in 1848 but the early 'fifties here were also a period of very high rates, as they were in Bavaria and in Prussia as well (see Figs. 2.3 and 2.6).

Patterns in property crimes in both of these national series, consequently, are quite suggestive. Trends in (and comparative levels of) property crimes appear to be consistent with explanations which link property crimes to urbanism or to the process of urbanisation-industrialisation, a problem which is taken up again in the final section of this chapter. However, several large cycles and periods in property crimes are apparent, some of which appear to have been international in scope and which beg explanation, and these are the focus of the following section.

Theft and Economic Conditions

Few modern observers would deny the existence of a rough correlation between severe economic crisis and theft rates; the huge peak in theft rates in both Germany and France in the 1840s, for instance, coincides with the greatest subsistence crisis of modern times in the Western world. But do more 'normal' cycles of crime correlate with subsistence costs or with general economic conditions? The debate has been spirited. Several causes of these disagreements have already been suggested. In the first place, the debate has not been without political overtones; a connection between theft and economic conditions or economic systems has often been advocated by the political left, and opposition to the theory has sometimes come from their opponents on the right. Also, most claims of no correlation have involved statistics from countries other than Germany and France, most notably from England and the United States. An old but frequently cited study by Dorothy S. Thomas, for instance, found no significant correlation between theft and the business cycle in England using correlation analysis, and this often has been used to refute the theory in general.[22] Relatedly, confusion has arisen because of differences in crime indexes. Broad indexes of total property crimes, the deficiencies of which have already been noted, have sometimes been utilised. Court records have frequently provided the basis for indexes and, while this is not necessarily a serious problem, they may react rather slowly to changes in rates due to the time lapse between the commiting of a crime and its coming to trial. Some studies have tried to take this into account by lagging crime statistics by a year or two, with mixed results. Similarly, economic indicators have varied. The older studies usually employed grain or bread prices, while more recent studies have sometimes used estimates of business cycles, unemployment, and so on. Some of these indicators are more accurate than others, and some are better indicators of actual material want than others. Moreover, the importance of these indexes as indicators of need and as determinants of crime may vary through time. Finally, differences in methods of analysis have caused misunderstanding. Time-series analysis is fraught with problems. Graphical analysis can be very subjective, but so can the determination of the trends which must be separated from the cyclical movement of indexes before more sophisticated correlational methods are used. Correlation coefficients for time-series are not, in other words, the exact mathematical measures that they appear to be.[23]

Some of these problems are virtually insoluble, but several steps have been taken to minimise them here. Due to the availability of long-term crime and economic indexes, the most practical units of analysis are national. While this necessitates partial reliance upon court records, the best indexes available have been used, including indexes of crimes reported to prosecutors rather than persons tried in France and indexes of persons tried rather than persons convicted in Germany. A wide range of economic indicators have been tested. Correlational analysis has been used to sort through these many variables, but graphical analysis has been utilised for more precise information about patterns of peaks and troughs. Recognising the limitations of time-series analysis, emphasis is upon whether a relationship exists and, if so, whether the relationship is positive or negative rather than upon an exact measurement of the strength of this relationship.

Coefficients of correlation between theft rates and a number of mainly economic indicators in France between 1831 and 1910 are provided in Table 2.6.[24] Indexes which indicate personal economic well-being as well as indexes which measure aspects of more general economic conditions have been tested. In order to check the possibility that effects upon criminal activity of changes in the economy were delayed and/or the possibility that the failure of crimes to come to trial during the year in which they were committed may have altered correlations (the index of reports to prosecutors which has been used is based in part upon cases tried), economic indicators were also correlated with theft rates from the following year.

Although there are some significant correlations in these lists, many coefficients are rather low. Moving theft rates back one year generally does not strengthen relationships, indicating that delays in the judicial system or in the effects of economic changes were not at fault. The best predictors of theft rates during the century as a whole were staple food prices; real wheat prices explain 37 per cent of the variance in theft rates while real bread prices explain 29 per cent.[25] Real wages were negatively associated with theft and explain about 20 per cent of the variance. Relationships between theft and individual indicators of general economic conditions were all low. It is worth noting, however, that theft related negatively to all indexes of imports and of production. Thus, while coefficients of correlations between theft and these economic indicators in general were not terribly high, several are significant and the signs of most coefficients are consistent with explanations linking high theft rates with economic hardship.

Table 2.6: Pearson Correlations Between Annual Theft Rates (Reports) and Various Economic Indexes in France, 1831-1910. Linear Trend Removed

Index Name	1831-1910[a]	1831-1910[a] theft lagged one year	1831-1869	1872-1910
Industrial price index	.16	.06	.33	−.09
Food price index	.32	.14	.48	.13
General price index	.26	.10	.42	.02
Real beef prices	.25[b]	.20[b]	.38[b]	.07
Real wheat prices	.61	.39	.75	.22
Real bread prices	.54	.30	.60	.40
Real rye prices	.17[b]	.35[b]	−	.17[b]
Real potato prices	−.10[b]	.36[b]	−	−.10
Potato consumption	−.05	−.42	−.31	.29
Wine consumption	−.60	−.46	−.66	−.56
Real wages	−.45[b]	−.21[b]	−.60[b]	−.32
Coal consumption	−.16	−.24	−.19	−.15
Iron production	−.14	−.23	−.11	−.19
Import, finished goods	−.12	−.08	−.21	−.07
Import, raw goods	−.20	−.22	−.38	−.10
Strikes	.45[b]	.48[b]	−	.45[b]
Strikers	.13[b]	.50[b]	−	.13[b]

[a]1870-71 excluded.
[b]Data available for only part of period.

One of the highest correlations occurred between theft rates and *per capita* wine consumption (r= −0.60). The correlation was negative, just opposite the result expected by nineteenth-century observers who frequently blamed increases in crime upon increased alcohol consumption.[26] Nevertheless, this should not be interpreted to mean that theft was prevented by increased alcohol consumption. Partial correlation suggests that this relationship is spurious and that the apparent relationship between alcohol and theft results from a direct link between prices and both theft and alcohol consumption. Wine consumption in France was positively related to real wages (r=0.46) and negatively related to food costs such as real bread prices (r= −0.42). When either of these indexes is controlled, the relationship between wine consumption and theft drops significantly.[27] Both theft rates and alcohol consumption

thus may have been influenced by cycles of prosperity and hardship,
though in opposite directions, and this would explain their tendency to
vary together.

In order to test the possibility that correlations for the entire period
1831-1910 camouflage changing relationships between theft and economic conditions, separate correlation coefficients were calculated
for the periods 1831-69 and 1872-1910.[28] The results of these calculations are revealing. The association between theft and economic conditions altered dramatically between 1831 and 1910. Whereas the
relationship appears to have been quite close before 1870, little
relationship between theft and economic indexes is apparent after 1870.
The low coefficients obtained for France for the entire period were due
to a loosening toward the end of the century of the association between
theft and these particular economic indexes.

During the early period, individual food costs again were the best
predictors of variations in theft rates. Real wheat prices explain 56 per
cent of the variance in theft rates between 1831 and 1869. Real bread
prices explain 36 per cent in this period compared to the 29 per cent
explained for the entire eight decades. Real wages now explain 36 per
cent of the variance in theft rates. During the second period, however,
the predictive power of food prices drops considerably. Coefficients for
real wheat prices drop to levels which are statistically insignificant. The
best predictor of theft rates among the food price indexes is real bread
prices, but this index now explains only 16 per cent of the variance in
theft. Clearly the association between theft rates and subsistence costs,
at least as measured by these specific indexes, weakened considerably
after 1870.

Graphs of real wheat and bread prices and of theft rates in Fig. 2.4
support and strengthen the conclusions reached through correlation
analysis, with but one modification. The agreement between theft rates
and these staple food prices was excellent before the Franco-Prussian
war. Nearly every peak and trough in theft rates during this period
coincides with a similar upswing or drop in the price of bread or wheat.
This includes the high peaks in thefts in 1847 and in the mid-1850s as
well as the trough in between; the high but short-lived peak in thefts
which climaxed in 1847 coincided exactly with a similar unusually
high rise in prices, while the high crime rates of the 1850s coincided
with an unusually high and long-lived upward bulge in prices. However,
the Franco-Prussian war and the accompanying change of régimes in
France does not provide such a clear line of demarcation as was earlier
implied. The correspondence between peak and troughs in thefts and in

prices continued for a time after 1872, but the association gradually loosened; after 1880, it was nearly absent.[29]

The agreement between patterns of theft and patterns of bread or wheat prices, even prior to 1870 or 1880, was of course not perfect. There were some small, independent movements in grain prices, such as the very small peaks and troughs which occurred in prices while theft rates were steadily rising between 1841 and 1844. In a few cases one index peaked or reached its trough before the other; the huge upswing in thefts during the early 1850s, for instance, peaked several years before prices did. Also, fluctuations in prices were usually greater in magnitude than those in theft rates, indicating that methods of recording and dealing with crimes had a levelling effect upon theft rates — the overall police system could not keep pace with price-induced theft in key periods — or that, as seems logical, the relationship between changes in prices and in theft was not one-to-one; a 50 per cent hike in prices, for example, though it would have been reflected in theft rates, would not necessarily have resulted in a 50 per cent increase in crime. Obviously, then, other influences besides wheat or bread prices were present, but these appear to have been secondary. In view of the excellent correspondence between rises and falls in thefts and in prices, it is reasonable to attribute a large part of the variation in French theft rates during the earlier period to fluctuations in the costs of staple foods.

The relationship between cycles in theft and in grain or bread prices in Bavaria (1835-60) and Prussia (1854-78) followed a pattern remarkably like the French during the same period; agreement between peaks and troughs in crime and in individual food prices was excellent, but with some hint of a declining correlation during the 1870s.

Graphs of theft rates and of grain prices in the portion of Bavaria lying east of the Rhine are provided in Fig. 2.5. All major moves in Bavarian theft rates, with the exception of a trough in 1843-4, may be explained by movements in grain prices. The hungry 'forties (and especially the high prices of 1846), the drop in prices that followed, and the recurrence of extremely high prices during the first half of the 'fifties clearly translated themselves into similar movements in theft rates. As in France, fluctuations in prices were of greater magnitude than those in theft.

Statistics of thefts and of prices for rye, wheat and potatoes in the eight 'old' provinces of Prussia (1854-78) fill in the gap between the end of the Bavarian statistics in 1860, and the beginning of national statistics in 1882 (Fig. 2.6). Here, too, the correlation between theft and individual food prices was high and positive. The correlation was highest for rye prices (r=0.77 or 59 per cent explained) and lowest for potato prices (r=0.67), but all correlations are quite high due to high correlations among prices. Thus the extremely elevated prices of the first three years of the period and the sharp drop that followed were clearly reflected in theft rates, as were the small hump in the first half of the 'sixties and the high peak of 1867-8. This pattern changed in the 'seventies, however. The three prices indexes began to move more independently of one another and, at the same time, the correspondence between theft rates and any one index became less close. The time period here is short; later Reich statistics will have to be used to determine whether this is the beginning of a trend. Nevertheless, the Prussian indexes after 1870 do seem to suggest the beginning of a more complex situation, with the predictive power of any single food price index being reduced.

The correlation between cycles in theft rates and in some individual grain or bread prices in the entire Reich between 1882 and 1912 was higher than in France during the same period, but was somewhat lower than in Bavaria and Prussia in the earlier period, and apparent again is a tendency for the relationship to loosen. As in Prussia, the highest correlation was with rye bread prices (r=0.61), although wheat prices (r=0.52) and pork prices (r=0.47) also correlated significantly. Figure 2.7 provides graphs of thefts as well as several grain and bread prices. A rough correspondence is apparent here between theft and grain prices, especially during the first part of the period. The long drop in theft rates until the end of the 'eighties did correspond to a period of declining grain and bread prices, the rise until the early 'nineties and the drop thereafter coincided roughly with the movement of grain prices, and a small peak in thefts in 1898 corresponded to a peak in grain and bread prices. There was also some correlation between peaks and troughs in thefts and in prices at the end of the period, although it was not high. As was the case in Bavaria and Prussia, then, theft rates were positively correlated with individual food prices but by now the relationship was no longer so close and, as in France, there is some evidence that the predictive power of these food prices continued to decline during this later period.

Coefficients of correlations between Reich theft rates and a variety of economic indicators are presented in Table 2.7.[30] Some of these correlations are quite high. As in France, however, the best predictors of theft were those indexes which directly measure the situation of the individual as opposed to more general business conditions. As was dis-

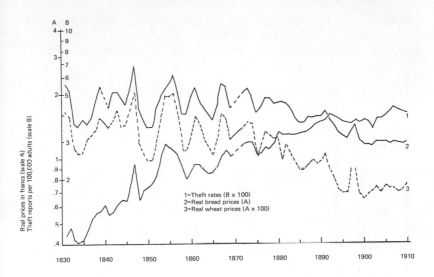

Fig 2.4: Rates of theft and real wheat and bread prices in France, 1831-1910

1=Theft rates (B x 100)
2=Real bread prices (A)
3=Real wheat prices (A x 100)

Fig 2.5: Theft rates and grain prices in Bavaria east
of the Rhine, 1836-60

Fig 2.6: Theft rates and food prices in the 'old' provinces of
Prussia, 1854-78

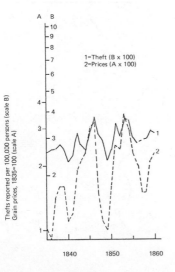

1=Theft (B x 100)
2=Prices (A x 100)

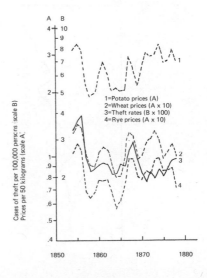

1=Potato prices (A)
2=Wheat prices (A x 10)
3=Theft rates (B x 100)
4=Rye prices (A x 10)

Persons tried per 100,000 adults
Real food price index

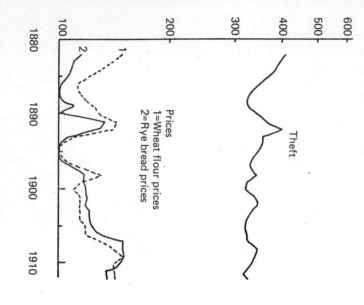

Prices
1=Wheat flour prices
2=Rye bread prices

Theft

Fig 2.7: Theft rates, wheat prices and rye bread prices in Germany, 1882-1912

Persons tried per 100,000 adults
Price indexes, 1895=100

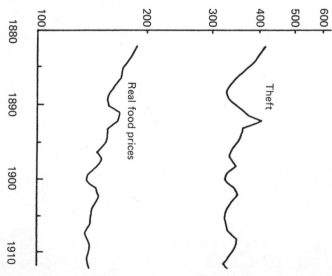

Real food prices

Theft

Fig 2.8: Theft rates and real food prices in Germany, 1882-1912

cussed above, individual food prices correlated positively and significantly with theft rates. Real wages correlated negatively and even more highly, explaining fully half of the variance in theft (r^2=0.50); this too is consistent with the hypothesised link between hardship and theft. Taken together, rye and wheat bread prices and real wages explain 81 per cent of the variance in theft rates.[31] And further evidence of a connection between theft and personal hardship is to be found in the positive relationship which obtained between theft and migration (r=0.61); migration tended to rise and fall with theft rates and, as the strong positive correlation between food prices and migration suggests (r=0.86), migration was more often motivated by need than by the lure of opportunity elsewhere.

Table 2.7: Pearson Correlations Between Annual Theft Rates (persons tried) and Various Economic Indexes in the German Reich, 1882-1910 Linear Trend Removed.

Index Name	1882-1910 r=	1882-1910 theft lagged 1 year r=
Pork prices	.47	.36
Potato prices	.16	.19
Wheat prices	.52	.55
Wheat bread prices	.10	.14
Rye bread prices	.61	.61
Cost of living index	.46	.48
Food price index	.57	.53
Real food prices	.75	.46
Wholesale food prices	.46	.50
Wholesale prices, general	.29	.61
Real industrial wages	−.71	−.55
Average income	.30	.35
Beer consumption	−.36	−.09
Potato consumption	−.28	−.30
Import, finished goods	.12	.21
Total imports	.26	.33
Import, raw goods	.10	.18
Industrial production	.17	.18
Iron production	.10	.15
Coal production	.29	.25
National income[a]	−.24	.01
Employment[a]	−.60	−.39
Migration	.61	.55
Strikes[a]	−.58	−.31
Strikers[a]	−.59	−.29

[a]Data series incomplete.

But the best individual predictors of fluctuations in theft rates were two indexes of real food prices. These indexes, which consist of weighted indexes of the cost of a typical grocery basket divided by industrial wages, estimate the cost of a total food budget and adjust it for income levels and are therefore the best available indexes of actual subsistence costs. Either of these indexes alone explains 56 per cent of the variance in theft rates.

This correlation is not so surprising, perhaps, given the correlations which obtained for individual food prices. What is especially note-worthy is the persistence of this relationship after the correlation between thefts and individual food prices had loosened. This is evident in the graphs of thefts and of real food costs in Figure 2.8. If slight differences in timing are ignored, the resemblance between the two indexes is remarkable. The long decline in thefts from the beginning of the period until the end of the 1880s was paralleled by a similar decline in real food prices, although prices reached their trough later than did thefts. The very high peak in thefts in the early 1890s coincided with a similar climb in real prices, but with prices peaking a year before thefts. Fluctuations in theft rates were less extreme after this, but continued to mirror fluctuations in prices fairly well.

Not every movement in theft rates can be explained by movements in real food prices, but then an estimate of real food prices cannot be expected accurately to measure personal well-being in all of its dimensions. At certain points where the correspondence between the move-ment of theft rates and of real food prices was less good, explanations may be possible in terms of movements in other economic indicators. The beginning of an upswing in theft rates in 1889 corresponded to the beginning of a drop in real wages; a small peak in thefts in 1898 lagged behind a peak in real food prices but coincided with a peak in the cost of living; the slight rise in thefts in 1906 corresponded to a small drop in real wages during that year. Thus the correlation between thefts and material well-being may have been better than any one index can measure. What is important here, however, is that a correlation between thefts and prices persisted throughout the period in Germany although, as will be discussed shortly, the specific determinants of cycles may have changed from mere subsistence costs to more general costs of living.

Several students of crime have claimed to find some relationship between property crimes and the business cycle.[32] To test this possi-bility, a number of indexes such as industrial production, imports, and national income were included in both the French and German correlational analyses. In neither country did these indexes correlate highly with theft rates.[33] The business cycle, however, is a composite of movements in a large number of indexes, and no single index provides an adequate measure. The lack of a strong relationship thus may be attributable simply to the inadequacy of these simple indexes of the business cycle. This possibility is difficult to test for France due to the lack of good, precise estimates of business cycles; lows in theft rates did not necessarily coincide with years identified as crisis years in general economic histories, but such labels are very poor and imprecise indexes of general economic conditions.[34] More precise periodisations are available for Germany, and these do indicate a relationship between business cycles and theft rates. Table 2.8 shows this relationship using a periodisation of the business cycle which divides the entire period 1882-1912 into periods of slumps and of upturn on the basis of a large number of economic indicators.[35] Four periods of slump and four periods of upturn are identified. Without exception, average theft rates during upswings were lower than average rates during slumps; thus periods of slump experienced rates of theft which averaged higher than the mean for the entire period while periods of upturn experienced theft rates below the mean.

Table 2.8: Average Theft Rates During Economic Upswings and Slumps in Germany, 1882-1912

Period	Phase of Cycle	Mean Theft Rate
1883-87	slump	365
1888-90	upswing	333
1891-94	slump	372
1895-1900	upswing	336
1901-02	slump	346
1903-07	upswing	326
1908-09	slump	347
1910-12	upswing	325

Mean theft rates 1882-1912=342
Mean theft rates during slumps=358
Mean theft rates during upswings=330

The business cycle can, of course, be dissected into more precise units than slumps and upswings. Five stages of the business cycle are in fact identified in Fig. 2.9: a slump phase includes both recession and primary rise, while upswing phases include secondary rises, boom years and capital shortages which precede or initiate a slump. In this graph, recessions are indicated by a steep drop in the line. Primary recessions, which represent slight upswings during a slump phase, are represented by small rises in the line while secondary rises, which represent more rapid upswings, are indicated by the steepest upward movement of the line. The turning-point at the end of an upswing, characterised as a capital shortage, is represented by a straight line. This graph, therefore, is very schematic and only the angles and timing of changes are important; no significance should be attached to absolute values or to the apparent trend in this graph of business cycles.[36]

With close examination, the inverse relationship between this line and theft rates is unmistakable. The recession of 1883 was not reflected in rising theft rates but crime dropped continuously as the economy turned upward in 1884 and more rapidly in 1888-9. The single exception here is a slight upturn in crime during the last year of this period. The sharp upswing in thefts in 1890-2 coincides with a capital shortage and the first two years of the slump of 1891-3. During the third year of recession, however, theft dropped considerably. With the exception of a small peak in 1898, theft dropped rather continuously during the slight economic upturn of 1894 and the rapid upswing of 1895-9. In 1900 came the end of the boom, and theft remained at approximately the

Fig 2.9: Theft rates and business cycles in Germany, 1882-1912. See text for explanation.

level of the preceding year. 1901 was a recession year; crime rates rose and continued to rise, though at a reduced rate, during the next year which, though still a part of the slump, represented a slight upswing after the recession. The years 1903-6 were boom years and crime rates generally dropped, with a slight rise in the last year. Theft remained fairly stable during the capital shortage of 1907, then rose as the economy entered a recession in 1908. The recession was short-lived, however, and after a slight upswing in 1909 the economy entered a boom phase which lasted to the end of the period. Theft rates dropped significantly in these years, but turned upward in 1912.

In only about six out of the thirty-one years between 1882 and 1912, therefore, can movements in theft rates not be explained by the business cycle; these include the drops in theft in 1883 and 1893 during slumps and the slight rises in crime during boom years in 1889, 1898, 1906 and 1912. Some of these exceptions, however, merely represent differences in timing in the two indexes, and most can be explained by movements in individual economic indicators. During the recession of 1883, for instance, real food prices were dropping so that this slump may not have resulted in as severe hardship as did most. Also, there are some indications that the characterisation of this year as a recession year may be misleading; total industrial production, total *per capita* production and *per capita* production of consumer goods all rose in 1883.[37] Movements in indexes such as food and real food prices likewise can be used to explain other exceptional fluctuations in theft rates, such as the drop during the recession in 1893 or the rise during the boom in 1912: real food costs dropped in 1893 in spite of the recession and both thefts and real food costs rose in 1912 in spite of the boom. Obviously, then, business cycles, or at least this particular characterisation of cycles, are inadequate to explain all of the movement in theft rates; at least for Germany, real food costs are a more precise predictor of theft cycles, and the fact that a rather close inverse relationship obtained between real food prices and the business cycle raises the possibility that the correlation between theft and the business cycle is spurious. Nevertheless, the predictive power of the business cycle is great, and this is true even at the end of the period.

That there was some connection between cycles in theft and in economic conditions in nineteenth-century Germany and France seems certain However, the specific determinants of theft cycles varied between the two nations and changed during the course of the century. Moreover, these variations parallel variations in diets and standards of living.

Until the last quarter of the nineteenth century, fluctuations in theft rates were closely related to fluctuations in the costs of basic staples. In France the correlation was highest for wheat prices, while in all three German series it was highest for rye or rye bread prices. This is consistent with what is known about diets and standards of living in this period. Life was marginal for many segments of the population, food costs made up a high percentage of personal budgets, and subsistence crises were frequent and, at least until mid-century, severe. *Per capita* income, however, was higher in France than in Germany, and this was reflected in diets; rye remained a basic staple among German lower classes long after it was being replaced by wheat in France. Thus the connection between thefts and costs of basic staples is reasonable, as are the national differences in the specific staple which correlated most highly.

The correlation between thefts and staple food prices declined in both Germany and France toward the end of the nineteenth century. This could be interpreted to mean that the connection between thefts and economics had loosened. However, in Germany cycles in theft paralleled fluctuations in the real cost of a total food budget as well as business cycles long after the correlation with rye prices had loosened, suggesting that subsistence costs were replaced by more general indexes of personal well-being. Toward the end of the nineteenth century subsistence crises became less frequent and less severe. Diets improved. Thus bread or grain prices no longer serve as reliable indexes of personal well-being.

The same phenomenon may explain the apparent loosening of the connection between theft and economics in France, although this is impossible to test due to the lack of good, general indexes like those available for Germany. Certainly, however, evidence is plentiful of a reduction in hardship, leading to more balanced diets, by the end of the century. Subsistence crises clearly were less frequent and less severe after 1850 than before, but there also seem to have been marked improvement after 1870. All indexes of real wheat and bread prices, for instance, dropped during the period (see Fig. 2.4). Fluctuations in the costs of these two staples also were less severe after 1870 than before.[38] As costs of basic foods declined and fluctuations diminished, basic diets may have become more diverse. As in Germany, a new pattern of criminal behaviour may have emerged as other indexes of personal hardship and prosperity took over the role played earlier by bread and grain prices.

If it is true that the economic determinants of theft changed in both countries, it is also true that France entered the second stage somewhat sooner than did Germany. Bread and grain prices in Germany after 1880 correlated much more highly with theft rates than they did in France during approximately the same period; the connection between individual food prices and crime loosened earlier in France than in Germany. This too is consistent with what is known about national patterns of industrialisation and subsistence. Germany entered the industrial revolution, with its accompanying disruption and hardship, much later and more violently than did France. German workers were also content with much less in terms of housing and diet than their French counterparts during the last half of the century. Also, grain and bread prices, although they may have fluctuated less frequently than in France, do not appear to have declined nor does the severity of fluctuations appear to have diminished after 1880 to the extent that they did in France (see Figs. 2.4 to 2.7). Consequently, the improvement in diets and the rise in subsistence levels may have come later in Germany than in France, causing the earlier pattern of criminal behaviour to last longer in this country.

Theft and Urbanisation

Both short- and long-term trends in national averages hinted of a correlation between theft and urbanisation. Regional statistics provide an opportunity to test this hypothesis further; the variety in patterns may have been related to differences in community size and growth. It should be noted, however, that the preceding statement actually raises two possibilities. Theft rates could have been related simply to community size *per se*, i.e. to levels of urbanism, as conventional wisdom presupposes; theft rates, then, should be higher in areas which were more heavily urban than in rural areas, and trends in theft should match quite closely trends in urban growth. On the other hand, however, theft rates may have been related to the fact of urban growth, i.e. to the process of urbanisation, rather than to community size as such. High theft rates, for instance, might have been due to the disruption and disorientations accompanying urban growth rather than to the nature of urban life. Theft rates may then correlate more highly with urban growth than with community size. Both possibilities need to be tested, and these two interrelated problems serve as the focus for the following discussion.

Two methods of analysis have been used here. The first relies upon a 'vertical' or cross-sectional cut in time; regional theft rates at a given point in time have been correlated with levels of urbanism, degree of urbanisation during the preceding years, and so on. For a 'horizontal' or longitudinal look at the movement of theft rates and of urban development through time, however, a number of areas have also been selected for closer examination. This 'case study' approach provides detailed information about trends in crime and in urban development, but also in some cases allows better crime indexes to be used than are available for a cross-sectional analysis; since trends rather than absolute levels of crime are being compared, uniformity in recording practices and legal definitions of crime is not so important here.

Urbanism and urbanisation are not, of course, the only possible explanations for regional crime patterns. High or rising theft rates may be part of the whole process of modernisation, including not only urban growth but industrialisation and the resultant changes in social and value systems. This possibility is difficult to test statistically due to the difficulty of constructing a valid index of modernisation. However, measures of industrialisation have been used here which, together with indexes of urbanisation, should provide at least a rough indicator of social change. In addition, numerous other possible correlates of theft rates can be conceived of; levels of crime could be related to cultural traditions or traditions of delinquency, to alcohol consumption, to standards of living, and so on. It is beyond the scope of this discussion to investigate these possibilities in detail but, where data were available, a variety of possible correlates of theft rates have been investigated briefly.

The French statistics available for a cross-sectional analysis have two serious shortcomings. Regional crimes statistics are limited to statistics of persons tried. They are thus subject to numerous distortions, including the possible urban-rural differentials already mentioned; upward trends in theft rates are likely to be underestimated or even ignored, especially in cities, and urban-rural differences in levels of property crime may be underestimated as well. Second, the smallest geographic unit for which statistics are available is the department. Such units are unfortunately rather large and often quite heterogeneous in structure. Departmental crime rates or urbanisation rates, like national rates, are often simply averages of diverse patterns; crime rates in a department which is predominantly rural, for instance, might appear high simply because of the existence of a town of modern size which had a high crime rate. Departmental statistics are far from ideal and must be considered as rough approximations subject to distortion.

On the other hand, though, these statistics were collected carefully and on a fairly uniform basis. Also, a great deal of demographic and economic data are available for the same geographic units. Without minimising their deficiencies, therefore, these statistics do lend themselves nicely to correlative assessment.

The basic mode of evaluation for the French statistics was a computer analysis of the relationship between theft rates and a number of economic and demographic variables from eighty-six departments around the turn of the century. Approximately forty original or constructed non-crime indexes were included, but factor analysis suggests that these can be grouped into measures of urbanism, urbanisation, industrialisation, alcohol consumption, food prices, and proportions of young people and of married men. Primary reliance is upon average theft rates per 100,000 adults between 1900 and 1904 and upon correlative data from approximately the same period. Average crime rates between 1838 and 1840 were used to measure departmental trends in crime and some correlative data from earlier periods were included in order to construct rough indicators of departmental social-economic change.

Table 2.9: Pearson Correlations Between Average Theft rates (Persons Tried) in French Departments 1900-4 and Various Demographic Variables

Variable Name	r	r^2
Population density	.15	.02
Urban percentage	.66	.44
Large urban (cities 10,000 +) percentage	.59	.35
Percentage of industrial workers	.68	.46
factory workers	.46	.21
Wine consumption per capita	−.03	−
Sex ratio (women per man)	.11	.01
Proportion of youth, both sexes	.23	.05
male	.28	.08
Percentage of married men	−.20	.04
foreign born	.41	.17
Illiteracy rate	−.09	.01
Unemployment 1901	.26	.07
Theft rates 1838-40	.21	.04
Change in urban percentage, 1876-1906	.55	.30
Percentage change in		
urban percentage 1876-1906	.12	.01
total urban population	.44	.19
total population	.49	.24
total population ignoring direction of change	.40	.16
population density 1876-1906	.46	.21
level of theft 1830s-1900s	.72	.52

The most significant results of this analysis are the correlations between theft and levels of urbanism and of industrialism (see Table 2.9).[39] Forty-four percent of the variance in theft rates is explainable simply by the proportion of the population living in cities in 1906 and 46 per cent by the percentage of the work force engaged in industry in 1901, two indexes which were highly interrelated (r=0.74 to 0.75). The percentage of the work force employed in large factories was less important (r^2=0.14 to 0.21). And even though cities or industrial areas did show some tendency to have a large percentage of their populations in crime-prone demographic groups (e.g. young males), the low correlations between theft rates and these demographic variables indicates that this cannot explain the connection between crime and urbanism-industrialism.[40]

The connection between theft and urbanism or industrialism can be more graphically shown by some more straightforward figures. Lowest average theft rates in France 1900-4 were experienced in Creuse, which was also the department which had the lowest proportion of its population living in cities of 2,000 or more persons; the department with the highest theft rates, Seine-Inférieure, was among the few departments which were more than 50 per cent urban. Theft rates in the 30 departments with greater than average proportions of their populations in cities averaged 68 per cent higher than in the less urbanised departments. Similarly, the 34 departments which had above average proportions of industrial populations had average theft rates which were 92 per cent higher than those in the other less-industrialised departments. And more detailed breakdowns of this data show that these patterns are not the result of a few unusual values.[41] Recorded rates of theft, then, did tend to be higher in urban-industrial areas than in rural-agricultural areas, and this in spite of a distortion in the records which would tend to minimise such differentials.

A relationship between theft rates and urban growth is also clear in these statistics; 30 per cent of the variation in theft rates, for example, can be explained by urbanisation rates, measured as the difference between the percentage of the population living in cities in 1906 and in 1875. But this does not prove that it was the process of urban growth which alone resulted in high theft rates. If it were the disruptions of urban growth rather than the fact of urban life which were responsible for high crime rates, the correlation should be higher and one also would expect the connection between theft and urbanism (or industrialism) to be non-linear, since middle-sized or smaller cities, in so far as they were likely to have higher growth rates than older urban centres, would tend to have higher crime rates. Yet a scattergram shows that the relationship os linear (Fig. 2.10). Thus the correlation between theft and social change, which is lower than for level of urbanism or industrialism, is at least partly derivative, reflecting the tendency of cities to have higher growth rates than the countryside.

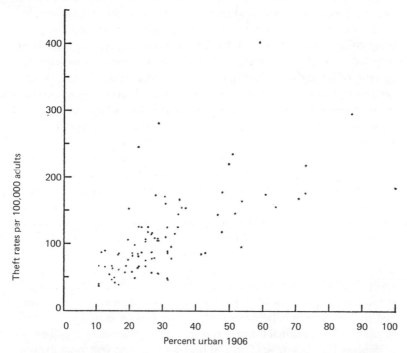

Fig 2.10: Average theft rates 1900-4 and percentage urban 1906 in France, 86 departments

Table 2.10: Breakdown of Average Theft Rates 1900-4 by Urban Percentage and Change in Urban Percentage 1876-1906 in French Departments

Departments With[a]	Number of Departments	Mean Theft rate
Low Urban Level, and		
Low Rates of Urban Change	37	79.7
High Rates of Urban Change	19	111.6
High Urban Level, and		
Low Rates of Urban Change	9	136.2
High Rates of Urban Change	21	159.2

[a]Low = below mean.
 High = above mean.

Still, it makes sense to use both urbanisation and urban levels together to explain theft rates. The breakdown of average theft rates by both percent urban and change in percent urban in Table 2.10 at least suggests this possibility. The 86 departments are classified into four groups here; these include less urbanised and relatively static departments, departments with low levels of urbanism but high rates of urban change, departments which were more highly urbanised but relatively static and, finally, departments which were highly urbanised but also grew rapidly between 1875 and 1906. As expected, average theft rates were higher in the more highly urban than in less urban areas, regardless of rates of urbanisation. But significantly, within each of these broad groups, urbanising areas had higher average theft rates than non-urbanising areas. While urban growth was less important than urban levels, urbanisation clearly made a difference in theft rates, though it was not a primary factor.

The results of the French cross-sectional analysis, then, can be summarised briefly as follows. The most important predictors of theft rates in France at the beginning of the twentieth century were measures of urbanism and industrialism. A direct connection between theft and urbanism, in fact, seems clear; as has usually been expected, theft rates did tend to be higher in urban than in rural departments, and this urban-rural differential would probably have been even greater with more adequate crime records. Departments which were experiencing high rates of urban growth tended to have higher crime rates than more static areas, but this variable was less important than community size and the connection between growth and theft rates should not be exaggerated. Put in personal terms, being in a city, rather than newly experiencing the disruptive effects of moving to a city, was more likely to make one a thief.

German data for a similar analysis are much less satisfactory than the French, and results of cross-sectional correlations consequently are less decisive; the highest correlation among a group of six demographic variables was a correlation of $r=0.38$ between the percentage of the population living in large cities in 1890 and the rate of serious thefts in 83 *Regierungs-Bezirke*[42] Other statistics suggest that this low correlation can be attributed to inadequacies in the data. Conviction statistics broken down by large *Stadtkreise* (city districts) and *Landkreise* (rural districts) or small *Stadtkreise* are available for some years, and in these a clear pattern emerges. Theft rates in major city districts averaged 378 convictions per 100,000 inhabitants in 1883-92, as opposed to only 273 for the remaining rural and small-town areas of Germany. Moreover, the relationship was linear; when major *Stadtkreise* are grouped according to size class, average theft rates increased along with community size (Table 2.11).[43] Most remarkably, though, these urban-rural differences in average theft rates were not the result of a skewed distribution; breakdowns by *Regierungs-Bezirk* according to *Stadt-* and *Landkreise* show that rates of convictions for theft were with but a few minor exceptions higher in large *Stadtkreise* than in other districts.[44] Thus definite urban-rural differentials in theft rates obtained in Germany as in France.

In addition to this cross-sectional analysis, a number of areas have been selected from both Germany and France for long-term comparisons. Due to the absence of local police statistics in France, the areas selected had to be departments and the crime indexes are court records. In Germany, however, police statistics are available for a number of urban as well as rural areas. These statistics give detailed information about the movement of theft rates through time in a variety of areas and thus provide a perspective absent from the cross-sectional analysis.

Eight French departments were selected as case studies. These fall into four basic groups on the basis of their experience with urbanisation and industrialisation during the nineteenth century. Creuse, Loir-et-Cher and the Vendée were predominantly rural, agricultural departments which did not urbanise or industrialise significantly during the century; population growth too was limited and, in fact, in both Creuse and the Vendée populations declined during part of the period. Pas-de-Calais and the Nord, on the other hand, represent areas which industrialised and urbanised massively during the last half of the century. Loire represents a traditional but still growing urban-industrial centre, while Seine (which includes Paris) and Bouches-du-Rhône (including Marseilles) were dynamic urban centres with long urban histories.[45]

Table 2.11: Average Theft Rates (Convictions) by City-Size Class in Germany 1883-97

Community Size Class	Average Theft Rate
Cities with populations of:	
50-100,000	318
100-150,000	329
more than 150,000	357
All cities with 50,000 population or more	341
All Germany	269
All but 55 largest cities	253

Statistics comparable to the French are not available for Germany; statistics of persons tried, which only began in 1882, were not broken down by smaller areas such as *Regierungs-Bezirke* after 1890. Conviction statistics, which are broken down regionally, are too problematic to be relied upon. Thus out of both choice and necessity, regional theft indexes for Germany are based upon police records, which are mainly available for cities or other relatively limited areas.

Rural indexes for Germany are somewhat scarce, especially toward the end of the century when most urban police statistics began. Gendarme reports from Württemberg between 1890 and 1913 are the best available because they approximate crimes reported rather than arrests and because they can be broken down into units smaller than the entire province.[46] This latter point is important. Although as a whole Württemberg was quite urban by French standards – one half of the population lived in cities by 1910 – the province was made up of four quite diverse *Kreise*. Neckarkreis was highly urbanised; almost 70 per cent of its population lived in cities in 1910, even when Stuttgart, Württemberg's leading city, is excluded. Population growth was also greatest here, although the growth rate was relatively low compared to most large cities (38 per cent, 1885-1910). Schwarzwaldkreis and Donaukreis were both moderately urbanised (about 43 per cent urban), though average city size was small, and both experienced moderate population and urban growth (20 per cent, 1885-1910) during the period. Jagstkreis was the least urban and most static *Kreis* during the period; 29 per cent of its population lived in towns and population growth was only 2 per cent between 1885 and 1910.[47] Thus, while none of the *Kreise* were as rural as the French departments of Creuse, Loir-et-Cher and Vendée, they do provide the closest possible approximation to a rural or small-town sample for Germany.

In addition, nine cities were selected for comparisons. For each of these cities, report statistics were available and, although the series differed somewhat in length, most fall roughly into the period 1880-1913. They are, therefore, roughly comparable to the Württemberg statistics. These cities can be divided into three groups. Urban centres which blossomed into large, dynamic industrial centres during this period include the Ruhr cities of Düsseldorf, Bochum and Duisberg as well as the small city of Oberhausen. Berlin and Breslau represent very large cities (2 million and ½ million inhabitants respectively in 1910) with long urban histories. Finally, Ohligs, Mülheim-am-Rhein and Bonn were less dynamic small cities in the western industrial area.[48]

The German samples are less neat than the French but have several advantages. Having been collected locally, the statistics are less directly comparable to one another than court statistics, although this is less troublesome for trend comparisons than for comparisons of crime levels. Time periods do not always coincide exactly. Selections must be made partly on the basis of availability of statistics. Truly rural areas are not really represented. Yet the statistics used are police statistics, and in most cases approximate statistics of crimes reported. The time-periods do coincide roughly and cover a period of substantial industrial and urban development. Finally, and perhaps most important, a range of city types is represented, including several large, new industrial cities.

One other group of German cases has been examined briefly. Conviction statistics for all property crimes between 1885 and 1905 have been compared for the two major Ruhr industrial *Regierungs-Bezirke* (Düsseldorf and Arnsberg), two agricultural areas adjacent to industrial areas (Minden and Hanover), a traditional urban centre (Berlin) and two remote agricultural districts (East Prussia and Pomerania).[49] These indexes obviously have many fallacies but, since they are based on court records, may be more directly comparable to the French indexes than are police statistics.

Significant differences are apparent in graphs of theft rates in the eight selected French departments (Figs. 2.11 to 2.14). Nevertheless, in broad outline trends and cycles in all departments were remarkably similar to trends and cycles in national rates. As for France as a whole, each department showed substantial increases in theft during the first half of the century, with severe fluctuations around the trend line occurring in the 'forties and especially the 'fifties. After about 1860 all departments experienced either decreased growth rates or actual declines in theft. In France as a whole this later tendency was attributed to a decline in the percentage of crimes reaching the courts, and this explanation probably applied to each of these departments as well. Trends after 1860, then, are almost certainly too negative in all departments, but this may be more true for rapidly growing and/or urban departments than for more stable rural ones. Trends in the eight departments during this period can be compared, but this distortion must be kept in mind.

With but few exceptions, differences in trends in theft after 1860 in these eight departments appear to be related to trends in social-economic structure. The three rural departments — Creuse, Vendée and Loir-et-Cher — all evidenced declining theft rates after about 1860 or 1870 (Fig. 2.11) and, with the exception of Seine (discussed later), were the only departments to do so. Levels of theft at the end of the period were

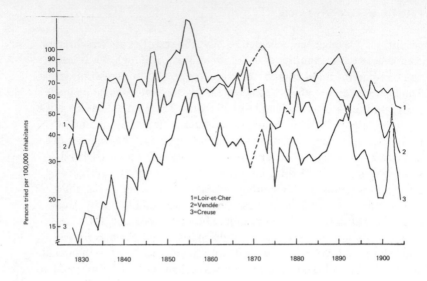

Fig 2.11: Theft rates in three rural departments of France, 1827-1904

Fig 2.12: Theft rates in a traditional industrial department of France, 1827-1904 (Loire)

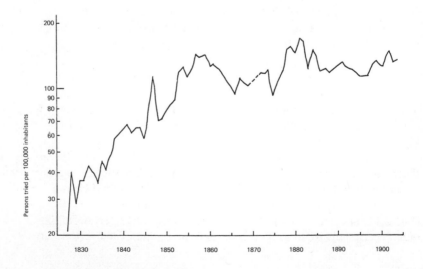

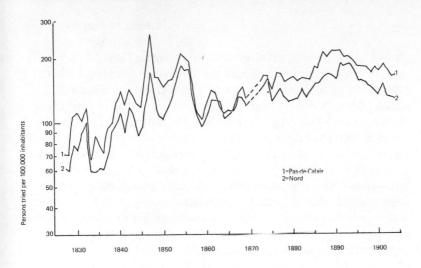

Fig 2.13: Theft rates in two new industrial departments of France, 1827-1904

Fig 2.14: Theft rates in two traditional urban departments of France, 1827-1904

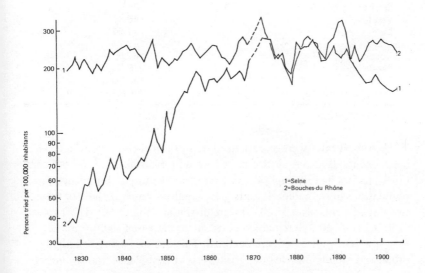

also far below those in the other five departments (Table 2.12). Moreover, among the three rural departments, rankings according to theft
rates coincided with rankings according to degree of urbanisation:
Creuse, the most rural department (10.8 per cent urban in 1901), had
the lowest theft rates while Loir-et-Cher, the least rural (19.7 per cent
urban in 1901) had the highest rates. Trends in theft in the three departments were too similar to risk such comparisons between trends. However, in all three departments population growth rates fell to very low
levels during this same period while theft rates were declining; each
department, in fact, actually lost population during part of the period.
And there is a rough correlation between the timing of declines in theft
rates and in population growth rates: the decline in theft rates is
apparent first in Creuse, where population growth began to fall off
earliest, while greatest declines in theft in Loir-et-Cher were experienced
after 1890, when actual loses in population took place in these two
departments. These indexes may overestimate the decline in theft rates.
Nevertheless, the fact that rural departments with relatively stable or
declining populations experienced stable or declining theft rates as well
as unusually low overall levels of theft is certainly consistent with
expectations.

Table 2.12: Average Theft Rates (Persons Tried) in Eight French
Departments 1900-4[a]

Department	Theft rate
Creuse	35.95
Vendée	48.53
Loir-et-Cher	72.54
Loire	162.78
Nord	167.56
Pas-de-Calais	219.80
Seine	183.60
Bouches-du-Rhône	296.96

[a]Per 100,000 adults.

High theft rates were experienced by both of the highly urban
departments; Bouches-du-Rhône, which with Marseilles was 87 per cent
urban, in fact had the highest theft rates in the sample. But although
populations in both departments grew rapidly, trends in theft in these
two departments after 1860-70 were dissimilar (Fig. 2.14). Theft rates
in Bouches-du-Rhône remained constant or increased slightly in the
long run, while rates in Seine declined. This decline in Seine, a highly
urban and rapidly-growing department, is at first glance hard to under-

stand. The long urban tradition may of course have mitigated the effects of urban growth here. More likely, however, a declining report-rate combined with special efforts at crime prevention worked together to produce this pattern. Overall crime rates were extremely high in Paris, and the complexity of crime detection and solution in this huge metropolis, attested to by virtually all observers, can only have increased during the course of the century. At the same time, the concern for order in the capital city led to special efforts to prevent and contain crime and disorder here; the special status of the Paris police organisation, which was responsible directly to the national government, was in fact due to such concern. Thus an increasing tendency to overlook minor crime and/or increasingly effective efforts at crime prevention may have worked to produce lowered − or at least apparently lowered − theft rates by the end of the century. And a similar though less pronounced phenomenon may explain the relative stability of theft rates in Bouches-du-Rhône. An increasing proportion of minor property crimes may have gone unreported due to high crime rates and the complexity of law enforcement in the large and traditionally lawless port city of Marseilles. At the same time, the importance of this city as well as its lawless tradition caused crime prevention to receive special attention here; the Marseilles police force was one of the few police organisations outside Paris to have a special relationship to the central and departmental governments.[50] Again, therefore, a falling report rate and/or increasingly effective efforts at crime prevention may explain the failure of crime rates to rise significantly in this growing urban department.

The greatest long-term increase in theft occurred in Pas-de-Calais (Fig. 2.13). This rise coincided with a period of massive industrialisation and urbanisation; although a predominantly rural department characterised by domestic and small industry in 1850, by the end of the century Pas-de-Calais was one of the leading textile and mining centres of France. By 1906, too, it was one of the few departments with 50 per cent of its population living in cities. A substantial growth in theft, then, is certainly consistent with expectations.

The Nord was also a leading industrial department by 1900 and, although it had more of a start in 1850 than did Pas-de-Calais, also experienced a massive transformation in approximately the same time period. The population of the Nord, which was dominated by mining and heavy industry, was more concentrated by the end of the period and grew more rapidly in the long run than did Pas-de-Calais, but its most massive population growth occurred before 1872; after this, population growth rates declined progressively while those of Pas-de-Calais increased. This may explain the fact that, in spite of its larger overall growth rate and higher level of urbanisation, long-term changes in theft rates were slightly less in the Nord than in Pas-de-Calais. In fact, a close look at the graphs suggests that during the first two decades of the period, while the Nord was growing most rapidly, trends in theft rates were quite similar to those in Pas de-Calais; after 1890, when population growth rates fell below those in Pas-de-Calais, theft rates fell and this explains the lack of a significant long-term upward trend.

The Loire, finally, was a traditional industrial centre which, although it eventually lost its place to the Nord and Pas-de-Calais, was still growing during the last half of the nineteenth century. The overall trend in theft here (Fig. 2.12) was very similar to that in the Nord, but the graph does not evidence the initial tendency to move upward which can be seen in the Nord. Levels of theft in the Loire were also quite similar to, though slightly below, those in the Nord. The behaviour of theft rates here, then, are roughly what might be expected of such a department.

At least in broad outline, the behaviour of theft rates after 1860-70 in these eight departments is consistent with patterns of urbanisation and industrialisation; urban areas had higher levels of theft than did rural, and growing urban-industrial areas experienced rising theft rates while those in stable rural areas appear to have fallen or remained stable. Only Paris did not fit this pattern, but there may have been extenuating circumstances here. Before 1860, however, comprehensible patterns are more difficult to discern in terms of change over time. Levels of theft do correlate rather well with levels of urbanisation in this period, as they did for the later period. Highest rates, at least around 1860, were experienced by Bouches-du-Rhône and the Seine, the two most urban departments, while the three rural departments evidenced the lowest theft rates; lowest rates of all, in fact, occurred in Creuse, the most rural department in the sample. But trends in theft do not group themselves so neatly. The most noticeable fact about trends in theft during this period is their similarity. Theft rates rose significantly in all areas, with no regular differences between urban and rural departments apparent. Two traditional urban-industrial areas, Bouches-du-Rhône and Loire, did experience the greatest increases, for instance, but rural Creuse's rate of increase was also high and the Seine's was not. Rates of increase in the Nord and Pas-de-Calais were similar to those in the rural departments or Loir-et-Cher and Vendée despite substantial differences in levels of urbanism or rates of urbanisation.

Trends in theft prior to 1860 thus do not appear to correlate with rates of urbanisation. Several extenuating circumstances need to be mentioned here, however. Even though some of these departments did not urbanise significantly in this period, all eight departments experienced significant population growth, resulting in younger populations and increased population densities.[51] Thus rates of urbanisation may not be the best measures of demographic change in this period. Also, all areas were massively affected by the subsistence crises of the 1840s and by the uncertainties of the 'fifties. 'Normal' patterns of criminal behaviour were upset by these extraordinary crises, and this affected short-run trends. Finally, rises in crime during this period, and especially during the early years, almost certainly reflected increases in report and trial rates as newly formed police departments and law enforcement agencies with new or expanded crime functions began to operate more efficiently. This would be especially true in rural departments where law enforcement agencies with criminal functions were minimal previously. These factors modify trends in such a way as to make correlations with rates of urbanisation before 1870 inconclusive.

We have, then, definite increases in property crime or its reporting in rural, old urban and urbanising areas. We have a further probability of particular increases in rates of change in the new urban areas. This would not necessarily bring them to the levels of the old city centres, for urbanness of whatever vintage is the prime variable here. For change, then, new urbanisation seems to be a real key. For overall levels, city size is the major variable. Only as new areas matched old in overall urbanisation, for example, would they rival them in theft rates.

Comparisons of court statistics in seven German districts (1885-1905) suggest patterns which are remarkably similar to those in France, and indeed bring out the basic patterns more clearly. Convictions for all property crimes in two remote rural provinces, in two newly industrial *Regierungs-Bezirke*, in two nearly agricultural regions and in one old city are shown in Figs. 2-15 to 2.18. As in France during the same period, property crime rates failed to rise in the two remote rural areas: rates remained about stable in Pomerania and actually declined sharply in East Prussia. Increases were sharpest in *Regierungs-Bezirke* Arnsberg and Düsseldorf, both of which were new and rapidly growing industrial areas in the Austrasian coalfield. The nearby agricultural *Regierungs-Bezirke* of Minden and Hanover also experienced increases, but these were less substantial. Property crimes rose in Berlin, but only slightly. In spite of the crudeness of these indexes, consequently, results are remarkably comparable to the French departmental comparisons, and

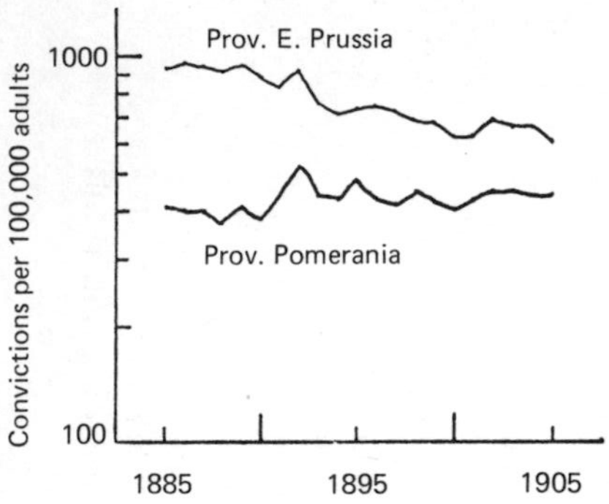

Fig 2.15

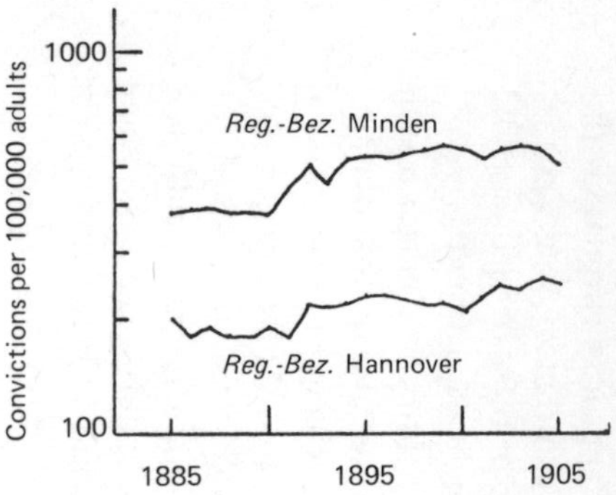

Fig 2.16

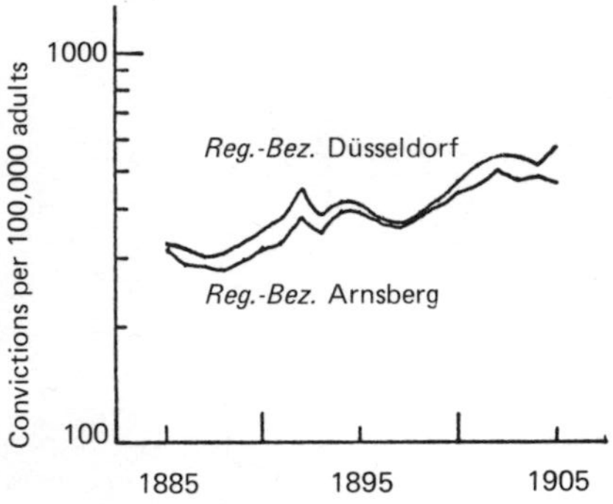

Fig 2.17

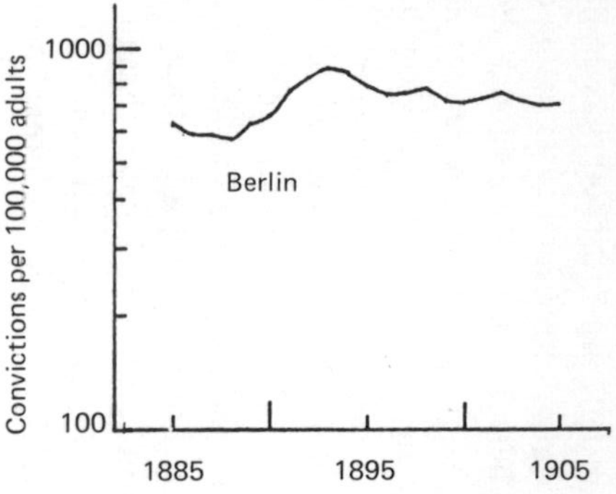

Fig 2.18

Figs 2.15 to 2.18: Convictions for all property crimes in seven districts of Germany, 1885-1905

this even includes the phenomenon of a capital city with a long urban history and a high population growth rate but a low rate of increase in crime rates.

An exact correlation between theft rates and community size or between trends in theft and urban growth rates cannot be claimed for the various Germany cities and *Kreise* included in Figs. 2.19 to 2.22 and Table 2.13. Nevertheless, when these areas are divided into two or three groups on the basis of city size (or urban percentage) as well as population growth rates, a pattern does become apparent. Theft rates were higher in large cities than in smaller cities or in rural and small-town areas; increases in theft rates were greatest in large and/or growing cities; and theft rises appear to have been related to urban growth.

Table 2.13: Average Theft Rates (Reports per 100,000) in Nine Cities and Four Rural or Small-town Districts of Germany 1905-9

	City size in 1,000's 1910[a]	Average theft rate	Rank by city size[a]	Rank by theft rate
Berlin	2059	1856.8	1	2
Breslau	512	2376.7	2	1
Düsseldorf	353	1724.4[b]	3	4
Duisberg	229	1211.9	4	6
Bochum	137	1498.6	5	5
Oberhausen	90	1759.8[c]	6	3
Bonn	89	1142.0	7	7
Mülheim am-Rhein	53	856.2	8	8
Ohligs	27	475.1	9	9
Neckarkreis	70%[d]	843.1	1	4
Donaukreis	43%	925.8	2	2
Schwarzwaldkreis	43%	874.4	3	3
Jagstkreis	29%	989.9	4	1

[a] Or urban percentage for Württemberg.
[b] 1903-7
[c] 1901-5
[d] Without Stuttgart.

By the end of the period, theft rates were without exception higher in large cities than in small towns or in rural areas and, moreover, were somewhat higher in the very large, old cities than in newer industrial cities (Table 2.13). This is significant, especially considering that these statistics come from local rather than uniformly collected national statistical records, and that thefts were more likely to be reported in rural areas than in cities. Within broad groups the correlation is inexact; theft rates were higher in Breslau, the second largest city, than in Berlin, for example, and were higher in Jagstkreis, the least urban areas of Württemberg, than in Neckarkreis which was 70 per cent urban. Among

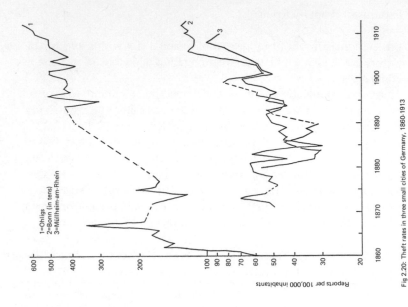

Fig 2.20: Theft rates in three small cities of Germany, 1860-1913

1=Ohligs
2=Bonn (in tens)
3=Müllheim-am-Rhein

Reports per 100,000 inhabitants

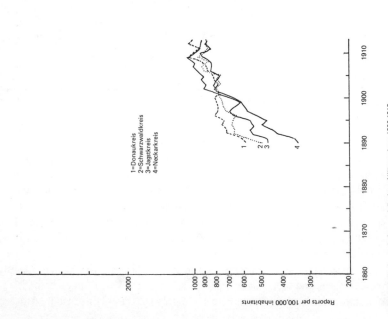

Fig 2.19: Theft rates in four rural districts of Württemberg, 1890-1913

1=Donaukreis
2=Schwarzwaldkreis
3=Jagstkreis
4=Neckarkreis

Reports per 100,000 inhabitants

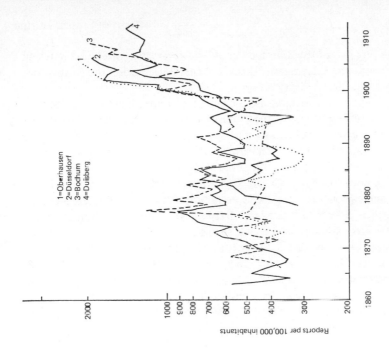

Fig 2.21: Theft rates in two old cities of Germany, 1881-1913

1=Breslau
2=Berlin

Reports per 100 000 inhabitants

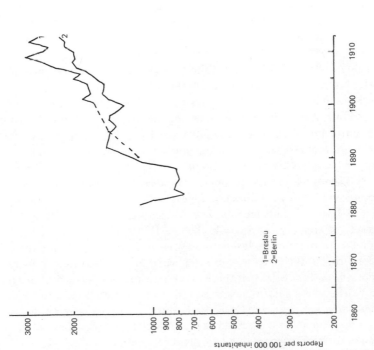

Fig 2.22 Theft rates in four new industrial cities of Germany, 1863-1913

1=Oberhausen
2=Düsseldorf
3=Bochum
4=Duisberg

Reports per 100,000 inhabitants

the three small towns in the sample, however, the correlation between city size and theft rates is exact. In general, therefore, the correlation between theft and city size is accurate.

Theft rates rose in all areas during the approximate period 1880-1910, but the slopes of these trends differed substantially. The steepest rise occurred in the cities with the greatest population growth, i.e. the new industrial cities.[52] The growth rate in Duisberg, however, was significantly less than in the other three industrial cities, in spite of a huge population growth rate, but similar to that in Bonn which, although a much smaller town, grew more rapidly than any of the remaining areas or cities. Theft rates rose less in Berlin, but population growth rates were also lower here and, as in France, the fact that this was the capital city may have led to extra efforts at crime prevention.[53] No significant differences in long-range trend are apparent between Württemberg and the smaller towns of Ohligs and Mülheim, in spite of the significant differences in population growth rates. Within Württemberg, theft rates rose most in Neckarkreis, the most urban and fastest growing of the four districts, but the second greatest rise was in Jagstkreis, the most rural and static district.

These estimates of long-term trends require qualification; in some areas, the rise was relatively constant over the entire period while in others it was concentrated at the end of the period. Theft rates rose fairly consistently in the four districts of Württemberg, in Berlin, and possibly in Breslau and Ohligs, although the last two series are incomplete. This was not true, however, in the other two small towns and in the Ruhr industrial cities. Here rates were relatively constant or, as in Düsseldorf, rose only moderately during the first half of the period, but then turned up sharply between 1896 and 1899. The climb was steepest for the four industrial cities, although it was also quite sharp but began later and was less distinctive in Bonn.

This sharp rise in these independent indexes, as well as its timing, requires explanation. It does not appear to have been a national phenomenon. National court records show no significant increase during this period and no unusual activity in the late 1890s. Theft rates in Berlin climbed out of a trough during these years and increased constantly thereafter, but the increase seems to have begun long before. Similarly, there is little to suggest that these years have any special significance in the Württemberg indexes; changes in the slope of trends seem to have occurred in Jagstkreis and Donaukreis, but the changes were rather slight and cannot be considered very significant. The increase and its timing, therefore, appear to be localised geographically (most of the city indexes come from the same general region, the western industrial area) or, relatedly, connected to a common experience shared by these cities. Material conditions do not seem to provide an adequate explanation. Indexes of prices and of wages do not suggest that this was a period of particular hardship; some price and cost-of-living indexes do show a small peak in the late 1890s and an upward trend thereafter, but estimates of real wages and real food prices indicate improvement during this period. Similarly, estimates of business cycles show that the economy as a whole was in an upswing at the time that theft rates turned upward. In the western industrial region particularly, the last decade of the century was a period of economic expansion. Unless a case can be made for a connection between rising theft rates and prosperity, therefore, a purely economic explanation does not seem likely.

A more plausible explanation involves the growth and expansion of these cities. Exact measurements of urban population growth are difficult due to changes in the areas of these cities. Also, since the only reliable data come from periodic census figures, the exact timing of changes in growth rates cannot be pinpointed. However, some estimates of population growth at five-year intervals with territorial changes excluded are provided in Table 2.14, and these do show a similarity between patterns of growth in theft and in populations. In the four major industrial cities, a major upturn in population occurred between 1895 and 1900, i.e. during the same period when theft rates began their distinctive climb.[54] The spurt in theft rates in Bonn which came somewhat later also coincided with a huge jump in population growth rates. On the other hand, the years 1895-1900 do not appear to have been distinctive periods of growth in the areas which did not experience sharp rises in crime. The population of Württemberg increased more rapidly after 1895 than in the fifteen preceding years, but the rate of growth may not have been unusual; the high rate of growth between 1875 and 1880 suggests that the fifteen years between 1880 and 1895 were a period of unusually small growth.

City population figures give the impression that the years 1895-1900, when the sudden rise in thefts occurred, were a period of unusual demographic and therefore also economic expansion. However, city populations are not always the most accurate indexes of either demographic or economic dynamism; the four industrial cities in this sample were all based primarily upon heavy industry, including mining, and thus undoubtedly included many non-resident workers and transients who would not be included in census figures. Estimates of regional industrial populations and of coal production, therefore, may provide

better indexes of growth here. These are provided in Tables 2.15 and
2.16.[55] Three of the cities — Düsseldorf, Oberhausen and Duisberg —
were located within *Regierungs-Bezirk* Düsseldorf. As these figures
show, the last decade of the century was a period of massive industrial
and demographic development in this region. Industrial populations
and coal production grew in most industrial regions of western Germany
(as well as in neighbouring French industrial departments), but only in
Regierungs-Bezirk Düsseldorf did the rate of increase in coal production
actually rise toward the end of the century, and this came during the
1890s when theft rates also increased. Growth rates for industrial populations remained quite steady here up to World War I while falling in
other regions. This period was less distinctive in *Regierungs-Bezirk*
Arnsberg which contained Bochum: industrial populations and coal
production both rose, but the rate of increase fell and there is little
distinctive about the 1890s. Heavy industry was less important in
Arnsberg, however, while Bochum was a mining town and this city and
its environs probably experienced growth rates similar to those in
Regierungs-Bezirk Düsseldorf. That the 1890s were a period of extraordinary demographic as well as economic growth is thus confirmed by
regional statistics, and that this expansion should be reflected in rising
theft rates is hardly surprising.

Table 2.14: Population Growth in Nine German Cities and Provinces,
1875-1910, Main Territorial Changes Excluded

| | Total increase in population × 100,000 | | | | | | |
	1875 to 1880	1880 to 1885	1885 to 1890	1890 to 1895	1895 to 1900	1900 to 1905	1905 to 1910
Berlin	1.56	1.86	2.61	1.09	2.04	1.46	0.48
Düsseldorf	0.14	0.20	0.29	0.32	0.38	0.39	0.54[b]
Duisberg	0.04	0.07	0.11	0.11	0.23	0.31	0.37
Bochum	0.05	0.08	0.07	0.06	0.12	0.16	0.19
Oberhausen	0.02	0.03	0.05	0.05	0.12	0.10	0.13
Bonn	0.04	0.04	0.04	0.05	0.06	0.31	0.07
Mülheim-am-Rhein	0.03	0.05	0.06	0.05	0.09	0.06	0.02
Ohligs	—	—	0.02	0.02	0.03	0.03	0.03
Württemberg[a]	0.80	0.15	0.28	0.26	0.70	0.60	0.98

[a] Without Stuttgart
[b] Territorial changes

Table 2.15: Percentage Change in Coal Production in Selected
Regierungs-Bezirke and Departments of France and Germany, by Decade

	1868/72-1878/82	1878/82-1888/92	1888/92-1898/1902	1898/1902-1902/12
Pas-de-Calais	131.1	78.6	61.7	38.7
Nord	33.1	29.1	20.7	19.7
Aachen	12.9	22.3	28.3	43.0
Düsseldorf	45.0	38.3	62.6	65.6
Arnsberg	89.6	56.3	48.4	35.1
Recklinghausen	281.9	265.0	128.9	113.6

Table 2.16: Percentage Change in Estimated Industrial Populations in
Regierungs-Bezirke and Departments of Germany and France, by Decade

	1860/61-1870/72	1870/72-1880/81	1880/81-1890/91	1890/91-1900/01	1900/01-1910/11
Pas-de-Calais	175.0	103.0	61.2	68.5	48.4
Nord	34.8	30.2	19.2	16.2	10.3
Aachen		21.6	25.4	22.6	21.9
Düsseldorf		40.7	44.3	50.4	44.2
Arnsberg		73.8	60.4	70.6	42.9
Recklinghausen		30.0	181.3	211.1	57.1

The case study approach, then, in general confirms the results of correlational analysis. In both Germany and France, theft rates tended to be higher in cities than in the countryside. Moreover, urban growth was accompanied by rising theft rates. Capital cities provided the main exception to this pattern, though more clearly so in France than in Germany, but it still can be argued that the long history of urbanism in these two cities mitigated somewhat the effects of urban growth, that the complexity of crime detection in large capital cities distorted indexes and, most importantly, that political pressures resulted in unusual and relatively successful efforts at crime control in capital cities. Community size and growth certainly were not the sole determinant of theft rates, but their importance seems unmistakable.

Conclusion

These results suggest that conventional wisdom about the behaviour of theft rates is partially right, partially wrong. Cycles of theft do appear to have been related to fluctuations in material conditions, and levels of as well as trends in theft were related to community size and growth. But there is little to suggest a strong relationship between theft rates and the process of urbanisation itself, and this lack of evidence is important. Many commentators on the nineteenth-century city have viewed urbanism with some alarm, seeing cities as chaotic jungles seething with crime, disorder and vice.[56] Urban growth bred social disorganisation and anomie; social disorganisation and anomie bred prostitution, crime and popular disorder. Several deficiencies in this view have already been noted in the previous chapter. The lack of evidence for a connection between theft and urbanisation *per se* is another. If it were social disorder and 'uprootedness' which breeds crime, one would expect crime rates to be higher in new and growing cities than in older, more static cities, and that theft rates in new and rapidly growing cities would rise at first, then begin to drop as the city came of age. Moreover, since most critics of the city — which, at least until very recently, has included most commentators on the city — would agree that property values were especially protected by the rural social order in the somewhat more idyllic age before massive urbanisation, it is precisely property crimes such as theft where the effects of social disorganisation should be most obvious. Yet no such pattern is apparent. There are a few hints that the process of change may have made some difference, most notably in some of the German data, but this factor is completely overshadowed by community size; urbanisation was accompanied by rising theft rates, but primarily because large communities tended to have higher theft rates than small, not because the process of change itself drove rates up. The primary causes of urban theft rates, then, will have to be sought elsewhere — in the increased opportunities for crime in the city, the greater difficulty of crime solution in a large community, or perhaps in the replacement of old 'rural' value systems by new, modern values, rather than in 'normlessness' and social disorganisation.

Likewise, the theory that theft is motivated by actual need, although less widely held than the disorganisation theory of the city, requires some qualification. There is, to be sure, some justification for explaining theft rates during the first half of the nineteenth century in this way; witness, for example, the concordance of a subsistence crisis and very high theft rates in the 1840s. But as a general explanation, the need argument has obvious inadequacies. The upward trend in theft rates itself belies this. In spite of the fact that all indexes indicate some lessening of the cost of subsistence and a general improvement in standards of living for many segments of the population seems clear by the end of the century — certainly no subsistence crisis equal to that of the hungry 'forties occurred after 1850 — theft rates moved steadily upward, finally reaching a peak, at least in France, which was higher than any previous level. Moreover, most students would now admit that rural poverty was at least as intense as urban by the end of the century; yet urban theft rates were usually higher than rural. Cross-sectional correlations between theft rates and the few economic indexes available were not high. And finally, the relationship between cycles of crime and indexes of the most basic subsistence costs loosened after about 1860. Almost no one would deny that material hardship was responsible for many thefts, but clearly this explanation alone is inadequate to explain the behaviour of nineteenth-century theft rates.

Many nineteenth-century commentators, and the middle classes in general, would have argued then that they were right all along — that it was 'cupidity' which motivated theft. And, while such a moralistic explanation is too simplistic, they at least may have been correct in pointing to the human psyche. For the apparent change in the economic determinants of theft in both Germany and France during the latter half of the nineteenth century suggests that, as in the Merton-Gurr argument outlined earlier, the sense of deprivation is relative rather than absolute. Men may steal because they are in need, but the assessment of need depends upon what they have been led to expect or desire. The incidence of theft is dependent in part upon the relationship between what is expected and what is actually attained, not simply upon outright hardship.

Which variable is the best predictor of theft rates will depend upon levels of expectations. During the first half of the nineteenth century, expectations generally were low; prior to and during the early stages of massive industrialisation incomes were low and variable, basic living costs were high and subsistence crises frequent. That prices of basic staples should have had an effect upon theft rates is logical. But the 1840s mark the end of large-scale subsistence crises in the Western world. Industrialisation, although it brought hardship, eventually also meant improvement for large segments of the population, especially after its early stages. Incomes rose. The price of basic staples fluctuated somewhat less from year to year than before and in the long run either remained steady or rose more slowly than wages. New industrial products become available to those who could not previously afford them. Democratic ideals spread. While this improvement in standards of living should not be overemphasised — certainly substantial segments of the populations in Germany and France still lived in poverty —

standards of living and thus expectations were quite clearly higher by the beginning of the First World War than they had been seventy years before. This is why prices of very basic staples such as bread were replaced as determinants of crime by more general economic indexes and since standards of living were higher and industrialisation began earlier in France, the change naturally occurred earlier there than in Germany. The changes in mentality, divorcing expectations from outright subsistence needs, followed the same pattern.

And the same general argument might be applied to the connection between theft rates and urbanism, a connection which increased as the older economic determinants of crime loosened their hold. Constraints are fewer, to be sure, in the city than in the countryside; there are more opportunities to steal in the city, less chance of being apprehended, and in general informal sanctions are replaced by less effective formal controls. Given the same tendency toward delinquent behaviour, then, an urban dweller was more likely to commit such a property crime than a rural dweller. At the same time, though, urbanisation has usually meant increased expectations; social classes tend to be more fluid in the city than in the countryside, contact between the rich and poor frequent, and the hope of advancement greater. The motivation to steal, therefore, was greater in the city because expectations were higher, and this became increasingly true as the industrialisation process matured.

If this interpretation is correct, what we have in fact witnessed during the nineteenth century, first in France, then in Germany, is nothing less than the transition from pre-modern or pre-urban to modern or urban criminal patterns. During the early part of the century, expectations in general were low and property was protected by village traditions and by informal controls upon behaviour; thus, at least outside large cities, theft rates were relatively low and fluctuations were closely related to actual subsistence crises. At the same time, the magnitude of these crises, in a situation of general demographic pressure, caused a rapid, general increase in rates. The transition from a pre-industrial to an urban, industrial society in these countries, although still incomplete by 1914, meant a new value system and a new social organisation as well as new and higher standards of living. A modern society implies — and, in fact, requires — rising expectations, a desire to acquire material goods, which was not characteristic of the pre-industrial mind. Modern industry, for example, would be unthinkable without growing markets and a work force motivated by the desire to improve itself; one of the first tasks of early industry was to teach workers to continue working beyond what was required simply to maintain previous standards of living. At the same time, modernity and urban life have usually implied fewer informal constraints upon the individual and, relatedly, a declining respect for the sanctity of property. Modernisation, in other words, meant rising expectations — expectations that society often was unable to fulfil — along with a reduction in constraints upon the individual. Beginning in the cities, these values and conditions gradually spread to the countryside. That new patterns of criminal behaviour accompanied these changes is hardly surprising. In urban areas, theft rates rose as cities grew; but such crimes also increased, although more gradually, in many rural areas as modern, urban values spread. The economic determinants of theft also shifted, reflecting higher standards of living and new values which were in part the result of the interrelated processes of industrialisation and urbanisation. New definitions of well-being thus sustained the increase in theft which earlier subsistence crises had first produced, though now at a more moderate rate. Thus the two main analytical problems of this chapter — the effects of economic conditions and of urbanism upon theft rates — are not so unrelated as they at first seemed.

Rising theft rates usually have been treated as a growing malaise, a sign of increasing rejection of society's values and a symptom of an illness in society. In fact, however, the new patterns of crime should not be seen as pathological but as symptoms of modernity. For not only do they grow out of and reflect basic characteristics of modern life, but they imply an acceptance of modern society's values — if not of society's norms governing methods of attaining them — on the part of offenders. Nineteenth-century theft rates reflect, in Merton's term, a state of anomie — an acceptance of prevailing social goals, but a willingness to use means which society considers illegitimate in order to attain these goals They thus also reflect both the successes and failures of nineteenth century society: they signify the spread of modern values and expectations but also the failure of nineteenth-century society to meet these expectations. High theft rates are not necessarily a permanent characteristic of modern society, but nineteenth-century patterns of theft are a sign that society was coming of age.

3 PATTERNS OF VIOLENT CRIME

Conventional wisdom about crime, as the last chapter demonstrated, has some basis in fact for crimes of theft; theft rates did rise during the last century and the rise appears to have been associated with urban growth. But can the same results be expected for criminal violence? Most people would answer in the affirmative, for the association between the city and violence runs deep. Although the Western world is now dominated by urban values and life styles, modern man is still afraid of the city.[1] Underlying this apprehension is a fear of violence. On the most basic, irrational level, the city brings forth images of faceless masses rushing to and fro, of dark streets where sinister villains lurk, of chaos and disorder which breeds violence. On a more reasoned level, this underlying negativism is reflected in much literature on urbanism; as noted earlier, the city is often said to be characterised by loosened social ties, by formal but rather ineffective social controls, by great social tensions, by irresistible temptations to do evil, by a frenzied and impersonal way of life. Such a situation is thought to encourage all sorts of delinquency, but especially violence: muggings, rapes, assaults, homicides as well as riots and protests. Consequently, urban growth is assumed to result in large and persistent increases in violence. That violence and conflict are more frequent in cities than in the countryside, that they have increased during the past two centuries, and that this increase can be attributed to the spread of urbanisation or, more generally, to modernisation are thus basic tenets of both popular and scholarly belief.

These tenets increasingly are being called into question. Several objections to the general concept of urban alienation have already been raised. Moreover, the link between violence and urbanism has never had much empirical basis and lately some evidence to the contrary has begun to surface for both collective and interpersonal or criminal violence.[2] Clearly, therefore, the assumptions about violence and its correlates need to be tested.

The possibility of a connection between crime and economic conditions, the other major focus of the previous chapter, seems less intuitively obvious for violence than it does for theft. Nevertheless, correlations between cycles in violence and in various economic indexes have occasionally been noted.[3] Explanations, however, are sometimes difficult; faced with such a correlation for Bavaria, Georg von Mayr was forced to resort to the 'wantonness, cruelty, passion and uncontrolled sex drives' of the population.[4] Such explanations are hardly satisfactory. More promising is what W.A. Bonger, in a now classic synopsis of the literature dealing with crime and economic conditions, in 1916 called vengeance arising out of economic troubles; a person who falls upon hard times often seeks revenge and thus turns to violence.[5] This formulation is, of course, highly simplistic but bears some similarity to the more recent frustration-aggression hypothesis which is currently receiving attention as an explanation for collective violence. As suggested in Chapter 1, with the recognition that aggression may be directed against substitute as well as against actual objects of hostility, the argument becomes a reasonable explanation for criminal as well as collective violence. And, since this explanation for violence is based upon the concept of expectations, the possibility arises that both crimes against property and crimes against persons might be brought together in one explanation. The cyclical behaviour of violence is thus worth investigating.

Two categories of violence have been chosen for primary examination here. An investigation of homicide, the most serious of violent crimes against persons, is of course unavoidable. However, while indexes of homicide are often considered to be the most reliable of crime indexes, they are not without problems. Relatively few numbers are involved in an homicide index, even on a national level, so that sampling errors are significant; a few cases overlooked or wrongly classified can affect indexes substantially. And the possibility of such errors is great. Homicides, though perhaps less than other crimes, are subject to arbitrary classifications: a charge of homicide can, under some circumstances, be changed to one of involuntary manslaughter and attempted homicides are sometimes classified with actual homicides. The index, in other words, is dependent to some extent upon the contingencies of classification decisions. Also, whether a case is reported as an homicide or as assault and battery depends simply upon whether or not the victim dies, which in turn is affected by such variables as the availability of medical facilities, and this again introduces an arbitrary element into an index involving relatively small numbers. For these reasons, homicide indexes are not the ultimate measure of violence that they are often assumed to be. International comparisons of crime levels may be more reliable for homicide than for any other category of crime, but year-to-year fluctuations are probably strongly affected by random errors, even on the national level. On the local or even regional level, homicide indexes are virtually worthless because of the minuscule numbers involved.[6] Nevertheless, even though the line between assault and homicide is less clear than is commonly assumed, indexes of homicide do provide the most precise available indicators of serious violence.

But the most useful index of criminal violence in general is assault and battery. Although the incidence of assault was usually somewhat lower than that of theft, it was a frequent crime; thus the problem of random errors inherent in small numbers is reduced. Also, assault and battery is a serious crime involving a confrontation between victim and offender but without the stigma attached to a sexual assault as far as the victim and the likelihood of reporting are concerned; thus its indexes may be considered relatively reliable.

The index is, of course, far from infallible. One possible distortion is especially germane here and bears repeating. The argument was made in Chapter 1 that interpersonal violence is more likely to be overlooked by official crime records in a traditional rural society than in a modern urban situation. With the increased impersonality and the concern for order which accompanied modernisation and population growth during the nineteenth century, however, the concern about — and intolerance of — violence increased, possibly leading to an increased report rate. For the purposes of this discussion, the potential consequences of this distortion are twofold. First, during the nineteenth century rural levels of violence may be underestimated relative to urban by most crime statistics. And second, the report rate for assaults may have risen somewhat during the century in all areas as population density increased, but more so in rapidly urbanising areas than in more stable rural or even urban areas. Thus the slope of trends in violence may be somewhat too positive, and this is especially true in newly urbanising areas. These distortions may not be too serious. The greater concern about violence in the city may have been partially offset by the increased difficulty of crime detection and solution in an urban environment. Still, the fact must be kept in mind that indexes of assault and battery may be biased in favour of conventional wisdom which associates violence with urbanism.

The first two sections of this chapter focus separately upon the behaviour of these two indexes of violence, i.e. assault and battery and homicide, in nineteenth-century Germany and France. But another problem must concern us here, too, and that has to do with the relationship between violence and property crimes. It is not enough, for instance, to know that crime was higher in the city than in the countryside; it is essential to know whether urban-rural differences in the balance or 'mix' of crimes obtained. Consequently, the relationship between these two categories of crime — theft and violence — is a recurring theme throughout the following discussion while providing the major focus for the third section of the chapter.

The discussion of violence and its correlates is necessarily complex. For the sake of clarity, therefore, the main substantive conclusions have been summarised briefly in the last section of this chapter. Also, as in the previous chapter, we have maintained a fairly clear demarcation between descriptive or correlative problems and problems of a more interpretive nature; although interpretive issues cannot be divorced from statistical analysis, they are dealt with more systematically in the chapter conclusion. Thus the reader may find it helpful to refer to this section before moving into the more detailed analysis in the bulk of the chapter.

Assault and Battery

Indexes of assault and battery reveal an increase in levels of interpersonal violence during the nineteenth century; rates of assault and battery rose significantly in France between 1831 and 1910, in Bavaria (1835-60), in Prussia (1854-78) and in Germany as a whole after 1882 (Tables 3.1 and 3.2).[7] A gross comparison of assault rates in Germany and France at the end of the period suggests a link between violence

Table 3.1: Rates of Assault and Battery in France 1830-1910, Averaged by Decade[a]

	Cases reported	Persons tried
1830s	69.2	57.8
1840s	81.4	63.2
1850s	80.6	60.9
1960s	89.1	73.1
1870s[b]	105.3	78.7
1880s	117.4	90.7
1890s	135.7	99.6
1900s	152.7	109.6
Change, 1830s–1900s	+121%	+90%
Change, 1840s–1900s	+88%	+73%
Change, 1880s–1900s	+30%	+21%

[a]Per 100,000 inhabitants.
[b]Excluding 1870-71

and modernisation. Assault rates rose in both countries between 1882 and 1910, but the increase was substantially higher in Germany (where rates rose 44 per cent), the more rapidly urbanising and industrialising nation, than in France (where rates rose only 30 per cent). Moreover, by the beginning of the twentieth century, assault rates in France, the less urban and industrial nation, were under half those in Germany, regardless of which of the two French indexes are used; between 1900 and 1909, an average of 369.67 persons were tried for assault per 100,000 punishable persons in Germany in contrast to only 109.61 persons tried and 152.70 cases reported in France.

Table 3.2: Rates of Assault and Battery in Germany, 1835-1909, Averaged by Decade

Bavaria[a]	
1835—39	46.0
1840—49	48.9
1850—59	61.7
Change, 1830s-50s	+34%
Prussia[b]	
1854—59	39.8
1860—69	51.2
1870—78	63.1
Change, 1850s-70s	+59%
Reich[c]	
1882—89	256.2
1890—99	348.2
1900—09	369.7
Change, 1880s-1900s	+44%

[a]Reports per 100,000 persons in the territory east of the Rhine. Exact category is crimes against persons resulting in death; assault represented 91% of this category in 1850.
[b]New judicial investigations per 100,000 persons in the 'old' provinces of Prussia.
[c]Persons tried per 100,000 punishable persons.

Such comparisons are far from conclusive for reasons that by now are obvious. To what extent, first of all, can these trends and international differences be related to urbanisation or modernisation as opposed to some other factor? Only a more detailed analysis of trends and comparisons of larger numbers of areas can begin to answer such a question. Secondly, to what extent are these apparent differences real? There are few specific reasons to doubt that rising assault rates reflect changes in the actual incidence of assault. It is doubtful that increases in rates of reporting could cause such massive and sustained rises as are indicated here, but the fact that German assault rates were higher than French might be partly attributable to differences in recording policies or to differences in legal definitions of assault and, as in the case of theft rates, this makes for a problem in assessment which is almost insoluble. The higher level of assault in Germany flies in the face of national stereotypes of the docile, law-abiding German. National stereotypes are of course dubious — but it could be argued that a greater concern about order and violence in Germany led to higher report rates, resulting in a higher apparent assault rate. And if the suggested urban-rural differentials in rates of reporting do hold true, a higher proportion of all violent crimes may have been reported in Germany than in France since Germany was more highly urbanised. That these factors are adequate to explain the huge difference between German and French assault rates is unlikely. Rates of assault probably were actually higher in Germany than in France by 1900; assault rates probably did rise in both countries during the century; and the rise at the end of the period likely was higher in Germany than in France. Nevertheless, conclusions about international differences in the incidence of violence, as well as about the causes of these differences, must remain tentative at this point.

Figs. 3.1 to 3.5 show that while the above estimates of long-range trends are basically correct, the slope of these trends was not constant. In France the increase in assault rates was massive — by the early 1900s, rates had reached a level 119 per cent higher than in the 1830s — and was spread throughout the entire century. A careful examination of Fig. 3.1 shows, however, that a single linear or even curvilinear trend for the entire century is unrealistic and that the century should be divided into three periods on the basis of trends. Assault rates moved steadily upward between 1831 and 1850, with only minor fluctuations. However, the last few years of this period coincided with the beginning of the largest single cycle of the century, in terms of both length and amplitude, and this represented a break in this early trend; assault rates moved upward rather sharply between 1847 and 1850, then quickly dropped by 1855 to a level almost as low as in 1831. A new trend line is possible after this point. Assault rates moved upward between 1855 and the end of the Second Empire at a more rapid rate than during any other period of similar length. The climb was continued after 1870, but at a rate slightly lower than that of 1831-48, and the rate of increase was quite constant from this point until 1910, when the index terminates.

The rate of increase in assault rates, in other words, was higher

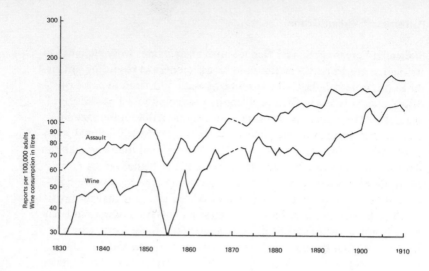

Fig 3.1a: Rates of assault and *per capita* wine consumption in France, 1831-1910

Fig 3.1b: Assault rates and prices in France, 1831-1910

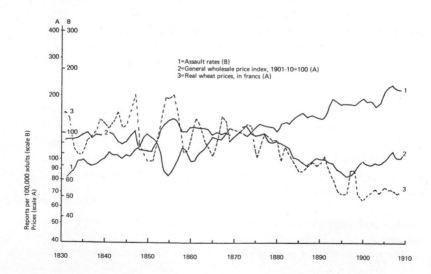

1=Assault rates (B)
2=General wholesale price index, 1901-10=100 (A)
3=Real wheat prices, in francs (A)

before 1870 than after, and higher between 1855 and 1869 than before 1855. The argument might be made that the rapid rise before 1848 and the even greater rise before 1870 reflect an atmosphere of escalating violence and disorder during the years preceding the revolution of 1848 and during the last years of the Second Empire. One would assume, then, that the years immediately following 1848 and 1870 would show a noticeable decrease in levels of violence, that is, a return to normalcy. This was not the case. No substantial drop in assault rates is apparent after 1870 and the fall after 1848 did not occur until several years later. Also, indexes of collective violence do not evidence a pattern of escalating violence which would support the hypothesis; the incidence of collective violence increased prior to both 1848 and 1870, but the peak around 1870 was not very high and in both cases this increase was a short-lived phenomenon.[8]

A better argument is that trends in assault rates reflected changes occurring in society and the economy. Urbanisation and industrialisation progressed fairly steadily during the nineteenth century in France, but the greatest impact was felt before 1870.[9] The fact that growth rates were higher for assault between 1831 and 1850 than after 1870 thus might be attributed to the high rates of social and economic change combined with the novelty of the experience during the early period. Moreover, the large increase in violence during the 1850s and 1860s parallels the tremendous urban and industrial expansion of the Second Empire; the era when rates of violence grew most substantially coincides with the most dynamic decades, in terms of urban and industrial growth, of the nineteenth century. On the other hand, though, assault rates after 1855 were climbing out of a trough and the high rate of increase in violence may simply reflect the tendency of crime rates to attain their original levels. Trends in French assault rates do nicely parallel trends in urbanisation, but the argument remains inconclusive.

The lack of a comparable index for the entire century makes a similar long-term analysis impossible for Germany. Rates of crimes against persons rose only slightly in Bavaria between 1835 and 1858, but industrialisation had only barely begun here and Bavaria remained predominantly rural throughout the period (Fig. 3.2).[10] In Prussia a substantial rise is evident, but the greatest increase occurred between 1872 and 1878 (Fig. 3.3). Most interesting, however, is the pattern in the Reich after 1882: the trend line for this assault index is curvilinear on semilogarithmic paper (Fig. 3.4). The rise in assault rates was quite steady and sharp during the first fifteen years of this series. After about

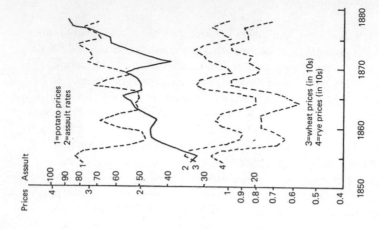

Fig 3.3: Rates of assault and food prices in Prussia, 1854-78

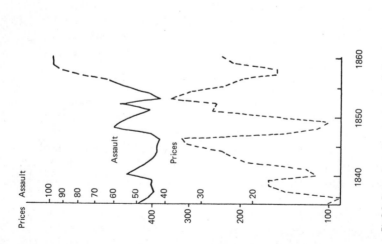

Fig 3.2: Rates of assault and grain prices in Bavaria, 1835-60

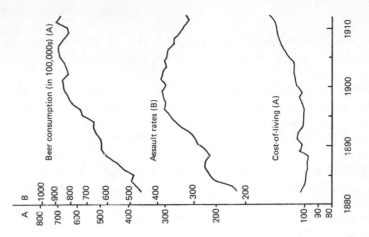

Fig 3.5: Rates of assault, cost-of-living and beer consumption in Germany, 1882-1912

A — Beer consumption (in 100,000s) (A)
B — Assault rates (B)
Cost-of-living (A)

Persons tried per 100,000 adults (B)
Cost-of-living index, 1895=100 (A)
Total beer consumption in 100,000's of hectolitres

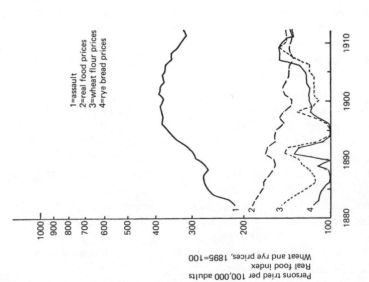

Fig 3.4: Rates of assault and food prices in Germany, 1882-1912

1=assault
2=real food prices
3=wheat flour prices
4=rye bread prices

Persons tried per 100,000 adults
Real food index
Wheat and rye prices, 1895=100

1896, however, the rate of increase began to fall off. After 1902 assault rates actually began to decline, and they continued to do so until the end of the series in 1912.

This pattern is highly suggestive. While no precise periodisation is possible due to the absence of national indexes before 1882, the steady upward climb in assault rates prior to the turn of the century parallels the modernisation process in Germany. The phenomenal industrial and urban growth of Germany during the last half of the nineteenth century is too well known to require documentation. But the levelling off during the late 1890s and the actual decline in assault rates after the turn of the century is interesting. Urban and industrial growth certainly did not slacken during these years, which witnessed the continued development of large-scale industry and large urban centres as well as the opening up of relatively new western industrial areas. If anything, the pace quickened during the 1890s: the proportion of the population living in cities rose almost twelve percentage points between 1890 and 1900, more than double the increase during any other decade between 1871 and 1910, while the output of pig-iron rose 83 per cent in the 1890s compared to only 71 per cent in the 1880s.[11] If trends in assault rates are to be explained by modernisation, therefore, it will have to be by the advent of modernisation rather than by the ongoing process. Violence, perhaps, increased initially due to the disruptions and/or tensions of social change, but decreased as change and modernity became less novel. Although French rates do not so clearly suggest this phenomenon, it might be argued that the gradualness of change in France as a whole coupled with the differences in timing of takeoffs in the various regions and industries caused the upward trend in violence to be sustained; and even here changes in *rates* of increase could relate to our hypothesis.

Levels and trends in national averages, then, can be linked to urbanisation in a general way. A further examination of this relationship follows later through analysis of regional rates. Before moving to regional data, however, a look at the cyclical behaviour of national indexes is in order.

Fig. 3.1 reveals significant cyclical fluctuations around the trend in French assault rates. In contrast to the theft index, however, no periodisation is possible on the basis of the length or amplitude of these cycles. Overall variance around the trend was higher before 1870 than after but this was due to the huge fluctuations between 1847 and 1855-7; with the exception of this large cycle, fluctuations were as great after 1870 as before.

The behaviour of assault rates during the crisis of the 'forties and during the early 'fifties is interesting. Theft rates, it will be remembered, experienced a sharp peak during the subsistence crisis in 1846-7, dropped to their previous level during the revolution of 1848, then began a long climb during a period of rising prices to a very high peak in 1854. At first assault rates moved similarly, rising slightly in 1847, but then they continued to rise throughout the revolutionary years. Assault rates peaked in 1850, while theft rates were in the early stages of a long climb, and then began to decline, reaching a very low trough in 1855, one year after the peak in theft rates.

The behaviour of assault rates during these years raises several interesting possibilities. First, the apparent relationship between cycles in theft and in assault during the 'forties and 'fifties suggests that theft and assault may have been inversely related to one another during the nineteenth century. Second, if this is true, assault rates also may have been inversely related to prices, since a positive relationship between theft and economic indicators such as prices has been found. Finally, the fact that the largest cycle in interpersonal violence coincided with the greatest period of collective violence during the nineteenth century suggests a possible relationship between these two phenomena.

The relationship between indexes of violence and of theft is discussed more completely later in this chapter but deserves brief mention here. Some observers have claimed to find an inverse relationship through time between violence and property crimes in a number of countries.[12] This does seem to have been the case for assault and battery in France prior to 1870 or 1880; before this time, a dichotomy between peaks and troughs in graphs of theft and of assaults is fairly clear (cf. Figs. 2.1 and 3.1). The length of the cycles as well as approximate coincidence of peaks in one index with troughs in the other indicates that this should be seen as an actual inverse relationship rather than a situation in which peaks in one index simply lagged behind those in the other. The relationship was most obvious during the large cycles in both theft and assault during the late 'forties and early 'fifties, but was present in other years as well.

However, this correspondence broke down after about 1880 and beginning in the 'nineties a positive relationship obtained.[13] The causes of this change are obscure, but it does at least refute any hypothesis that the two crimes are inherently inversely related; theft does not necessarily take the place of violence, and conversely, violence does not necessarily displace theft. Rather, the breakdown in the correlation suggests that both theft and violence were influenced, though in

opposite directions, by a third variable during the early period but that
the connection between this independent variable and one or both of
the crime indexes changed later.

The relationship between assault rates and economic conditions
followed a similar pattern. Correlation coefficients for a number of
economic indicators are shown in Table 3.3.[14] Correlations between the
assault and most indexes of production or imports were quite low, with
the single exception of imports of finished goods, an index which may
provide a fair index of general prosperity since imports of finished
goods are especially sensitive to cycles of prosperity and hardship. While
the correlation between assault and this index was only moderate, it
was positive and, during the first half of the century, alone explained
40 per cent of the variance in assaults. However, coefficients for most
price and wage indexes were considerably higher. Correlations with
price indexes were negative while a positive relationship obtained with
the index of real wages. Lagging assault rates by a year does not, in
most cases, improve correlations and in all cases coefficients were considerably higher before 1870 than after. The general price index, in
fact, explains a full 77 per cent of the variance in assault rates before
1870 as opposed to only 3 per cent in the later period, and the predictive power of several other price indexes in the earlier period is almost
as great. Violence thus seems to have had some positive relationship to
prosperity, but the link underwent a change that very roughly recalls
the periodisation of theft rates and their correlates. Here are two major
hypotheses to be tested and explained.

The graph in Fig. 3.1 bears out this relationship and periodisation.
Prior to 1870, most major peaks in real wheat prices, for instance,
corresponded to troughs in assault rates, and vice versa, and the timing
is almost exact. The largest cycle in assault, i.e. that which occurred
during the late 'forties and 'fifties, is entirely explainable by this price
index. The rise in assault rates between 1847 and 1850 corresponded
to a sharp decline in wheat prices, the sharpest of the century. The peak
in violence in 1850 corresponded to the bottom of the trough in wheat
prices. Wheat prices remained at this low trough for a year while assault
rates began moving downward, but then the inverse relationship continued. Assault rates reached their trough in 1855, then moved upward;
grain prices neared their peak one year earlier but reached the absolute
peak in 1856, then started downward. Timing was not always exact,
therefore, but no particular pattern of lagging is apparent and the
differences are trivial. In most cases, absolute peaks and troughs correspond exactly. And only two major peaks in grain prices before 1870
were not clearly reflected in assault rates: a small peak in 1839 occurred

during a period of rising assault rates, and the sharp peak in prices in 1847 coincided with but a tiny trough in assaults. Otherwise, the correspondence was good.

Table 3.3: Pearson Correlations Between Annual Rates of Assault and Battery (Reports) and Various Economic Indicators in France 1831-1910. Linear Trend Removed

	1831-1910[a]	1831-1910[a] assault lagged 1 year	1831-1869	1872-1910
	r=	r=	r=	r=
Industrial price index	−.51	−.52	−.85	.05
Food price index	−.58	−.51	−.75	−.38
General price index	−.60	−.58	−.88	−.17
Real wheat prices	−.60	−.49	−.65	−.50
Real bread prices	−.60	−.45	−.61	−.65
Real rye prices	−.16[b]	−.05[b]	−	−.16[b]
Real potato prices	.04[b]	−.27[b]	−	.04
Potato consumption	.24	.44	.31	.15
Wine consumption	.65	.51	.86	.42
Coal production	.46	.54	.48	.45
Iron production	.34	.41	.14	.54
Import, finished goods	.44	.44	.63	.29
Import, raw materials	−.05	−.07	−.28	.11
Import, industrial goods	.10	.08	.01	.16
Real wages	.50[b]	.28[b]	.77[b]	.49

[a]1870-1 excluded.
[b]Data available for only part of period.

But this ceased to be true after 1870. Although small peaks in grain prices corresponded with troughs in assaults in some years, the movement of the two indexes was quite independent throughout the remainder of the century. A similar pattern also held for the general composite price index.

The argument might be made on several grounds that the relationship between assault and prices is an illusion. One possibility is that drops in violence during hard times in the early periods of high prices by of police activities; being preoccupied during period of high prices by rising theft rates, reports of assault may have been ignored. Later in the century police forces improved and were better able to handle increases in crime so that rises in theft did not have such an effect. Several objections to this explanation may be made, however. Usually crimes of violence have been considered more serious than property crimes in Western society; thus one would expect crimes of violence to have received prior attention, and report rates for theft should have been affected by levels of violence, not the other way round. Secondly, although police efficiency did improve during the nineteenth century due to advances in forensic science and improved communications, some signs that population growth as well as rising crime levels were straining police forces by the end of the century have already been noted. Consequently, one would expect the inverse relationship between violence and thefts or prices to return toward the end of the century. But this did not happen; instead, a slight positive relationship obtained. While the explanation cannot be entirely discounted, variations in police activities and effectiveness are insufficient to explain this pattern.

Another possibility is that cycles in violence were affected by alcohol consumption, which in turn was influenced by price levels. This explanation is not unreasonable; during the nineteenth century increases in violence were frequently blamed on alcohol, and some more recent studies have added support to this explanation.[15] In order to test this possibility, statistics of annual wine consumption per inhabitant were included in the correlational analysis. The result produced the highest correlation in the program; a positive correlation of r=0.65 was obtained for the entire series, and r=0.86 (r^2=0.74) for the period 1831-69. An examination of the graph of wine consumption in Fig. 3.1 confirms this pattern. The correspondence between peaks and troughs in wine consumption and in assault before 1870 was excellent — almost perfect. The relationship loosened after 1870, as the correlation coefficients suggest, but this does not mean that the correlation between violence and alcohol consumption disappeared. Significant instances of coincidences between peaks and troughs in the two graphs do remain. And, even though France is famed for its wines, the index of wine consumption is by no means a totally adequate index of alcohol consumption. Recent investigations, in fact, suggest that other forms of alcohol such as *apéritifs* were beginning to displace wine in France by the end of the century, and the loosening connection between wine and violence could simply reflect a change in drinking habits due, in part, to higher standards of living.[16]

This high correlation suggests a number of interesting possibilities. To be sure, the apparent relationship between wine consumption and violence could be spurious, reflecting the impact of prices upon both violence and wine consumption independently. However, the correlation between violence and wine consumption (r=0.65) was higher than either the correlation between violence and prices (r= −0.60) or between prices and wine consumption (r= −0.36), which is inconsistent with this hypothesis. Also, when prices are controlled using partial correlation, the correlation does not drop substantially as it should if the relationship were spurious.[17] Another obvious possibility, of course, is that prices operated indirectly through alcohol consumption to affect assault rates; when prices dropped alcohol consumption rose, leading to an increase in assaults. This hypothesis too is not supported by available statistics. The correlation between violence and prices does not drop significantly when wine consumption is held constant as it should if wine consumption were an intervening variable. Also, it would seem that the correlation between prices and wine consumption should have been higher than it was.

Neither of these possibilities can be discounted completely by these statistics. The method of extracting trends which was used here is somewhat crude, for instance, so that the results of partial correlation for these time-series are not completely firm. Also, any single price index hardly provides a complete index of material well-being; thus the connection between wine consumption and prosperity may have been closer than these statistics reveal. And a model involving only three variables may be too simple.

Nevertheless, correlation analysis points toward two other interrelated possibilities. Both prices and wine consumption may have affected violence independently. Together, then, using multiple regression, wine consumption and the index of general prices explain 70 per cent of the variance in theft during the century as a whole, and the proportion explained would increase considerably if only the period 1831-69 were used.[18] However, the apparent relationship between violence and alcohol consumption may still have been spurious, but the result of a third independent variable other than prices. Alcohol consumption, rather than affecting assault rates directly, could rather have reflected the same underlying factors or situations which led to violence. Assault and alcohol consumption, for instance, may both have been expressions of the same underlying social tensions and conflicts. Or increased leisure time or the relative absence of financial worries may have led to more interaction between people — including more time spent in bars — and thus would have set up situations which were conducive to both alcohol consumption and interpersonal violence. Thus a direct causal connection between alcohol consumption and violence is far from proved.

The third issue raised by the behaviour of assault rates during the 1840s and 1850s has to do with the possibility of a connection between criminal and collective violence. A comparison of these assault indexes with Charles Tilly's estimates of disturbances in France, however, suggests only a rough and limited correspondence at best.[19] The late 'forties and early 'fifties were periods of high rates in both indexes, of course, but little correspondence between actual peaks and troughs in the two indexes is apparent. No significant correlation between major cycles in collective and interpersonal violence is evident for the rest of the century either; the second largest cycle in disturbances, which occurred between the end of the 1890s and the First World War, does not seem to have coincided with any unusual movement in assault rates, for instance. Thus, while there was a rough similarity in the behaviour of the two indexes during one extreme crisis, no significant correlation between assault and collective violence can be claimed for the century as a whole.

Turning to Germany, one is again plagued by the lack of a unified, long-term, national series. A comparison of assault rates in Bavaria (1835-60), in Prussia (1854-78) and in the entire German Reich (1882-1912) suggests a dampening of fluctuations after 1882; while rather large fluctuations around the trend are apparent in both early indexes, only very slight yearly variations occurred in the Reich index after 1882 (see Fig. 3.2 to 3.4). The most significant cycle in the Reich index was a small upward bulge beginning in 1884 and reaching its trough in 1888. Otherwise, fluctuations were very small indeed.

Whether this dampening of cycles represents an actual change in crime patterns is debatable. Local indexes of assault reports during the same period show much greater variability but they, like the early Bavarian and Prussian indexes, are based on smaller numbers, thus more variability is to be expected. Since the Reich index is based upon court statistics, however, the argument could be made that the processes leading up to trial in Germany may have had a levelling effect which tended to dampen year-to-year changes in the number of persons brought to trial. Cases are not necessarily brought to trial in the year that they occur and perhaps in Germany trial dates tended to be adjusted to even out court loads.

As in France, the behaviour of assault rates during the 1840s and 1850s suggests the possibility of a correlation with collective violence. Bavaria, the largest area for which good statistics are available during this period,[20] can hardly be considered representative of Germany as a whole: as noted, it was predominantly rural and agricultural during this period, emancipation of serfs had hardly begun by 1848, guild restrictions had only recently been loosened and, though a wave of disturbances did sweep Bavaria in 1848, no actual political revolution occurred.[21] Thus Bavaria stands in contrast to France during this period. Nevertheless, the behaviour of Bavarian assault rates was remarkably similar to the French. As in France, the period was characterised by a large upward bulge in assault rates, in terms of length and amplitude, beginning in 1847 when theft rates were dropping. The peak came earlier and, though high, was less extraordinary and was shorter-lived than in France: Bavarian assault rates peaked during the 'revolutions' of 1848, dropped to a trough in 1851, then moved to a smaller peak in 1852.

The possibility of a long-term relationship with collective violence is difficult to test because of the absence of regional statistics of collective violence prior to 1882 and because of the small number of disturbances after this time; according to Richard Tilly's estimates, the maximum number of disturbances in any single year after 1850 was less than twenty.[22] What little evidence exists does not suggest any consistent relationship, however. Peaks in assault rates in Bavaria and in Prussia do not coincide consistently with peaks in disturbances in Germany as a whole. The same is true for the Reich indexes after 1882 though again the insignificance of fluctuations in national assault rates and the small number of annual disturbances hamper comparisons. Relatedly, the lack of correlation is apparent for strikes as well (r=0.05), where substantial numerical rates of protest are involved. We emerge, then, with a pattern of non-connection paralleling that of France.

The relationship between cycles in theft and in assault also follows a pattern like that in France; an inverse relationship obtained between the two indexes during the earlier years of the century, but lessened as the century progressed. In Bavaria, peaks in thefts tended to coincide with troughs in assault and vice versa, between 1835 and 1860 (cf. Figs. 2.3 and 3.2). When theft rates peaked in 1846, for instance, assault rates were in a trough and theft rates then dropped while assault rates rose to a peak in 1848. The major exception to this pattern was a peak in theft in the mid-1840s which was not reflected in crimes against persons. This negative relationship is less apparent in Prussia after 1854 (Figs. 2.6 and 3.3) and was totally absent in the Reich (Figs. 2.2 and 3.4) as well as in local city indexes after 1882; after 1882, in fact, there is slight evidence of a positive relationship for some areas.[23]

A similar periodisation holds for the correlation between economic conditions and assault rates. In Bavaria between 1835 and 1860 a clear negative relationship obtained between cycles of assault and grain prices. Peaks in grain prices in 1846 and 1853 coincided with troughs in assault rates, for instance, and the peak in assaults during 1848 occurred

when grain prices were almost at the bottom of a very low trough
(Fig. 3.2). Likewise in Prussia after 1854 a negative relationship was
apparent between cycles in assault and in prices of rye, wheat and
potatoes until about 1870, but not after that time (Fig. 3.3).[24] There is
only the slightest evidence of a relationship between assault and a
variety of economic indicators in the Reich after 1882 (Figs. 3.4 and
3.5).[25] Movements in cost-of-living and wheat indexes, for instance,
operated quite independently; if there was any inverse relationship at
all, it was very slight and limited to the first years of the period. And
this lack of a negative correlation at the end of the period was not
simply due to the inadequacies of national court records since it is also
apparent in several Ruhr cities for which both police and price statistics
are available.[26]

An index of beer consumption in the Reich is included in Fig. 3.5.
As in France during the post-1870 period, no significant correlation
between fluctuations in violence and in alcohol consumption can be
seen here. Unfortunately, the lack of good alcohol consumption
indexes for Prussia and Bavaria does not allow this possibility to be
tested for the early period.

For the century as a whole, then, the pattern of cycles in assaults
was remarkably similar in the two countries. In both Germany and
France, fluctuations in assault rates were negatively related to cycles
in theft and in economic hardship during the first half of the century,
with correlations loosening after 1870 and disappearing entirely later in
the century. The movement of assault rates was quite similar in France
and Bavaria around 1848 and correlated roughly with large cycles in
collective violence, but otherwise little connection between criminal
and collective violence was apparent in either country.

In neither Germany nor France do statistics of assault and battery
lend any support for the argument that interpersonal violence served
as a direct substitute for collective protest or violence. The broad
positive correlation between assault and battery and collective violence
during the 1840s and '50s, however, does leave open the possibility that
both collective and criminal violence may have been alternate expressions
of the same underlying tensions and conflicts during this early period,
though the participants in the two types of activities probably differed.
The lack of evidence for any relationship between the two phenomena
during the remainder of the century is not necessarily telling; until the
rise of strikes around 1900, collective violence was too localised and
infrequent for analysis on the national level to be very fruitful.

Moving from national to regional figures, one is immediately struck by considerable diversity; regional deviations from national levels and trends were somewhat less for assault than for theft, but still substantial. Distributions in both countries were positively skewed due to a few areas with extremely high crime rates. The range of rates was greatest in Germany. Here assault rates ranged from 80.47 per 100,000 punishable persons in the district of Dresden in 1885-90 to the phenomenal high of 704,06 in the Bavarian Palatinate.[27] In France the range was from 37.06 in Tarn-Garonne to 346.26 in Corsica. And in France, where long-term series are available, trends in assault rates show similar diversity; the rise in assault rates in Meurthe-et-Moselle was four times that of the nation as a whole while in Lot assault rates actually declined 54 per cent between 1838-40 and 1900-2. Here, the deceptiveness of national averages is clearly demonstrated.

The possibility that this variety in assault rates was due to differences in levels of urbanism can be eliminated quite easily. Correlations with measures of population density and of the proportion of the population living in cities (as well as in large cities only) were low and insignificant in Germany between 1885 and 1890 (r= —0.10 to —0.14). When assault rates in *Stadt-* and *Landkreise* are compared, no pattern of differences is apparent; rural rates were higher than rates in nearby urban areas in as many cases as they were lower.[28] And little correlation between rankings according to urbanism and assault rates is evident for the thirteen German areas selected as case studies in Table 3.4

And the same is true for France. The eight departments selected as case studies do give some hint of a relationship during the first half-century: Paris had the highest levels of violence and the three rural areas the lowest. But the rankings changed later, with rates in Paris falling drastically while levels in urban Bouches-du-Rhône fell below those in several less urban departments (Figs. 3.6 to 3.9 and Table 3.5). Pearson correlations for all 86 departments 1900-4 show only minor correlations between assault rates and measures of population density or the proportion of persons living in urban or even in large urban areas (r= —0.08 to 0.16). In short, these statistics provide no evidence of any relationship between urbanism and assault rates, in spite of a probable bias in crime records in favour of such a relationship, and thus the hypothesis must be rejected.

Evidence of a connection between urban growth and assault rates is mixed. German cross-sectional data do not reveal any relationship at all; the correlation between average assault rates 1885-90 and changes in the proportion of the population living in cities between 1875 and 1890 in the 83 *Regierungs-Bezirke* was in fact slightly negative (r= —0.13).

Table 3.4: Rankings by City Size and Average Assault Rates 1906-10 in
Nine German Cities and Four Small-town Districts of Württemberg

	City size 1910 in 1000s	Assualt rate 1906-10[a]	Ranking by city size	Ranking by assault rate
Berlin	2059	311.9	1	9
Breslau	512	487.8	2	3
Düsseldorf	353	321.1	3	8
Duisberg	229	384.4	4	6
Bochum	137	639.1	5	2
Oberhausen	90	1180.6	6	1
Bonn	89	463.1	7	4
Mülheim-am-Rhein	53	350.8	8	7
Ohligs	27	423.4	9	5
Neckarkreis	70% urban[b]	397.1	1	2
Donaukreis	43%	280.0	2	4
Schwarzwaldkreis	43%	414.8	3	1
Jagstkreis	29%	312.2	4	3

[a]Exact periods vary slightly; report rates per 100,000 persons. Württemberg:
reports by gendarmes only.
[b]Without Stuttgart.

Departmental statistics for France at least hint at a connection. The
forty departments with higher than average urbanisation rates between
1876 and 1906 experienced assault rates which were 39 per cent higher
than in those departments with lower than average urbanisation rates.
Relatedly, average violence rates in both rural and urban areas with high
urbanisation rates were higher than those in more static departments,
regardless of whether these were urban or rural.[29]

   None of the indexes in the French correlation programme described
in the last chapter in fact correlated very highly with assault rates (see
Appendix). The highest correlations were revealing, though they
pointed in somewhat contradictory directions; for if one of the correlations was with the change between 1876 and 1906 in the proportion of
the population living in cities, the other was with the assault rate
during the 1830s. Each of the variables alone explains about 20 per
cent of the variance in assault rates (r=0.44 – 0.45) and together, using
multiple regression, they explain 34 per cent of the variance.[30] The two
most important predictors of assault rates in this set of variables, then,
were rate of urbanisation and traditions of criminal violence, measured
as the level of assault at the beginning of the period. But it is vital to
note that the influence of urbanisation was not terribly great and that its
importance was in fact slightly less than that of traditions of violence.
   The correlation between proportions of young males and assault

rates was almost as high as for urbanisation (r= 0.36). The percentage of young men also correlated with rates of urbanisation so that the possibility that one of these relationships — either between assault and urbanisation or between assault and young men — was spurious must be considered. However, the correlation between the two demographic variables was not terribly high (r= 0.41) and the fact that the correlation was greatest between urbanisation and assault suggests that this latter relationship may have been primary. The presence of unusually high numbers of young males, a crime-prone age-group, in urbanising areas may have been partly responsible for higher assault rates here, but this is not sufficient to explain the relationship between violence and urban growth.

Table 3.5: Rankings by Urban Percentage and Average Assault Rates 1900-4 in Eight French Departments

	% urban 1901[a]	Assault rate 1900-4	Ranking by % urban	Ranking by assault rate
Seine	100.0	50.1	1	6
Bouches-du-Rhône	85.3	108.7	2	3
Nord	69.5	138.9	3	1
Loire	51.8	87.3	4	4
Pas-de-Calais	45.2	137.5	5	2
Loir-et-Cher	19.7	47.5	6	7
Vendée	13.6	42.7	7	8
Creuse	10.8	60.0	8	5

[a]Urban = population centres of 2,000 or more persons.
[b]Persons tried per 100,000 persons.

Measures of the level of industrial development correlated moderately with assault rates (r= 0.40 to 0.42). Industrial departments, however did tend to be those which had experienced the greatest urban growth (r= 0.57) and this may explain the connection. Total alcohol consumption also correlated moderately with assault rates (r= 0.41) and since the relationship was positive this appears consistent with previous correlations through time. Again, though, this does not prove a causal relationship.

The evidence from these cross-sectional breakdowns for a connection between assault and urbanisation, then, is not terribly strong; no relationship was apparent for Germany and, though a moderate relationship obtained in France, the connection was complicated by a number of factors. The biggest single cause of variation in assault rates remains regional tradition, which urbanisation could modify but not displace.

But a number of deficiencies in this analysis have already been pointed out; departments or *Regierungs-Bezirke*, for example are too large and heterogeneous for useful comparisons. Moreover, the indexes used here did not provide any useful measure of the novelty of urbanisation, a factor which the behaviour of national assault rates suggested might be important. This possibility, therefore, is best tested by examining the behaviour or assault rates in individual districts through time.

Among the eight selected French departments, assault rates were higher by 1900-4 in urbanising and industrialising areas than in the most urban and in strictly rural departments. By far the highest rates of violence were experienced by Pas-de-Calais and the Nord, the two newly-industrialised areas in the sample (see Table 3.5). Next highest was Bouches-du-Rhône, an old but rapidly growing urban commercial centre. Assault rates in Loire, a traditional but still dynamic industrial area, were somewhat lower while lowest rates were experienced by the Seine and the three rural departments.

Graphs of assault rates in Figs. 3.6 to 3.9 suggest a correlation between trends in violence and in urban-industrial development which is compatible with these findings. The highest growth rates for violence during the nineteenth century were in Pas-de-Calais and the Nord, and changes in the slope of trends here were roughly coincident with changes in rates of urban-industrial growth. Unlike the other departments in this sample, the most rapid increases in violence in both departments occurred between 1855 and 1870, the period when large-scale industrialisation began. Moreover, it could be argued, depending upon precise interpretation of the graphs, that the increase began slightly earlier but was less rapid in the Nord where industrialisation also began earlier. In both departments the rate of increase tapered off after 1870, when urban and industrial growth was less novel, and both graphs hint of a further decline in growth rates or perhaps even the beginning of an actual decline in violence during the last decade of the period.

The Loire too experienced a rapid climb in assault rates prior to 1870 which tapered off thereafter. The growth rate after 1870, however, was less than in Pas-de-Calais and the Nord while the increase between 1831 and 1869 was spread out over the entire period instead of being concentrated at the end.

Trends in the two traditional urban centres differed from one another though significantly neither department experienced substantial rises in violence. Seine, in fact, experienced an actual decline in assault rates during the century. As has been suggested for theft, a concern about disorder and especially violence in the nation's capital led to more effective law enforcement here than elsewhere and thus may have resulted in greater crime control. Moreover, the Seine's long urban history may have served to dampen the effects of urban growth here. These factors may also explain the failure of assault rates to rise substantially in Bouches-du-Rhône. Here violence did increase, but the rise was moderate. Significantly, most of the rise was concentrated after 1870, during a period when population growth rates were still high and when Marseilles was experiencing a great influx of dock and other unskilled workers, a group within which the risk of violence is usually assumed to be rather high.

Violence rose somewhat in the long run in the three rural departments of this sample, but much less than elsewhere. Although the evidence is sketchy, there is in fact some hint of a correlation between rising violence and the failure to grow demographically in Creuse and Vendée; several rises in violence at least coincided roughly with periods of least population growth.[31]

Assault rates in these eight French departments thus do show a tendency for rises in violence to accompany urban and industrial growth, but with one qualification. The early stages of this growth seem to have made the most difference in the incidence of violence; the connection seems to have loosened after the most difficult transitional stages of social change and, although evidence on this point is inconclusive, rates of violence may actually have declined after a period of adjustment.

As we can now expect, a comparison of assault rates in the thirteen selected German cities or districts does not reveal a simple relationship between levels of assault and past levels of urban growth (Table 3.6). True, the highest assault rates by the end of the period were in Bochum and Oberhausen, two of the most rapidly growing cities. But the other two cities in this category, Düsseldorf and Duisberg, ranked much lower; rates in Düsseldorf, in fact, were below those in several rural districts of Württemberg. Since these indexes come from local sources which were not collected on a uniform basis, such comparisons are far from conclusive. Nevertheless, these results are consistent with the contention that the mere fact of urban growth is insufficient to explain levels of violence in the nineteenth century.

Assault rates rose considerably in all these areas during the period for which statistics are available (Figs. 3.10 to 3.13). However, trend patterns were complex and evidence for a connection between urban

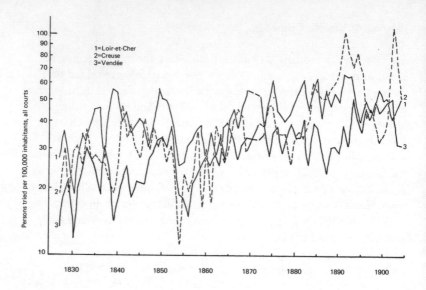

Fig 3.6: Assault rates in three rural departments of France, 1827-1904

Fig 3.7: Assault rates in two old urban centers of France, 1827-1904

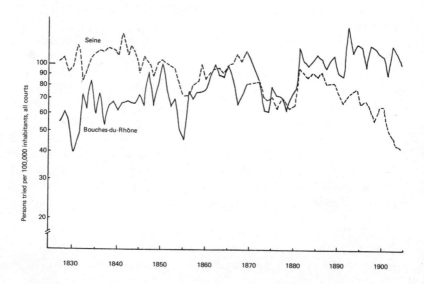

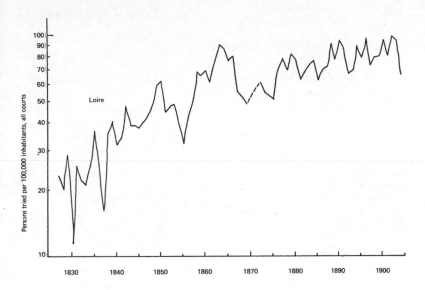

Fig 3.8: Assault rates in a traditional industrial department of France, 1827-1904

Fig 3.9: Assault rates in two new urban-industrial departments of France, 1827-1904

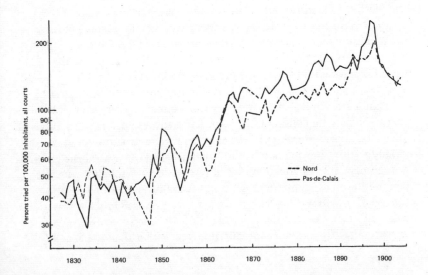

growth and rising violence is conflicting.

Table 3.6: Rankings by Average Assault Rate 1906-10 and Population
Growth in Thirteen German Communities

	Ranking by % population growth 1885-1900	Ranking by average assault rate 1906-10[a]
Duisberg	1	8
Oberhausen	2	1
Bochum	3	2
Düsseldorf	4	10
Bonn	5	4
Mülheim-am-Rhein	6	9
Ohligs	7	5
Breslau	8	3
Berlin	9	12
Neckarkreis[b]	10	7
Schwarzwaldkreis	11	6
Donaukreis	12	13
Jagstkreis	13	11

[a]Crimes reported per 100,000 persons (for the four *Kreise*, crimes reported to gendarmes only). Exact periods vary somewhat.
[b]Without Stuttgart.

The greatest and most consistent growth in violence occurred in Oberhausen, the newest industrial city in the sample. As late as 1871 Oberhausen had only 13,000 inhabitants. Industrialisation brought rapid growth, however; by 1905 the population had reached 52,000 and, with the incorporation of surrounding areas, it numbered 90,000 by 1910. Urbanisation was a new experience, therefore, and a massive rise in assault coincides with the transformation of a small town into an industrial city. No tendency for rates to level off by the end of the period is apparent, but by 1910 urban growth was still a novel experience and the stabilisation, if it occurred, probably came later.

Assault rates in Duisberg also suggest a connection between violence and urban growth. Duisberg too was a small town which grew rapidly under the impact of industrial development. Here assault rates grew rapidly at first after the late 'sixties, then levelled off toward the end of the century.[32] The plateau in assault rates coincided roughly with the period of most rapid urban growth, but it can be argued that by this time such growth was no longer new, especially since Duisberg was a larger city than Oberhausen from the start. Once again assault rates appear to have risen due to the initial impact rather than the absolute amount of urban growth.

The only other area for which crime data are available before about 1880 is the small town of Ohligs in the neighbourhood of Solingen. Although Ohligs did experience growth – the population doubled between 1885 and 1910 – it had only 27,000 inhabitants by 1910. After an initial rise in the 'fifties and 'sixties, rates of assault appear to have remained relatively constant here.

The pattern of violence in the three communities for which long-term crime series are available, therefore, is consistent with the hypothesised link between rising assault rates and the initial stages of urbanisation. Trends in assault in the nine remaining cases, however, provide only limited evidence for such a link, though the lack of crime indexes during the earlier stages of economic and demographic growth is a critical problem. Assault rates rose somewhat in all of these areas after 1880 or 1890, but the overall growth rates do not appear to have been connected with the speed of urbanisation; the rise in Berlin, an old city, was for instance greater than that in Düsseldorf or Bochum.

What is most notable about these graphs, however, is the similarity of many of them to the pattern which was observed for Germany as a whole (see Fig. 3.4); in the majority of these communities, assault rates moved up significantly at first, then at a reduced rate, and finally levelled off or actually declined. To be sure, the timing was not always the same; the levelling off occurred earlier in Düsseldorf than in Berlin or Württemberg, for instance. And there were exceptions, apart from those already mentioned: rates rose somewhat less in the same town of Bonn than elsewhere, with most of the rise coming at the end of the period, while rates in Bochum also rose but fluctuated so widely that an estimate of trend is difficult.

But in general the similarity is striking, providing a pattern which seems to have been almost a national phenomenon, and which returns us to hypotheses about its relationship to urbanisation and industrialisation. Trends in some areas were obviously consistent with our suggestion that novelty rather than urbanisation *per se* had greatest impact. Düsseldorf, for instance, was a rather large city before the massive industrialisation of the 1880s and '90s; that the levelling off should have come earlier there than in Württemberg or the small town of Mülheim-am-Rhein is reasonable. And the fact that similar patterns are evident for other areas which were not new urban centres does not necessarily negate the hypothesis. Berlin, for example, did experience substantial growth toward the end of the century and the influx of large numbers of unskilled and rural workers must have caused adjust-

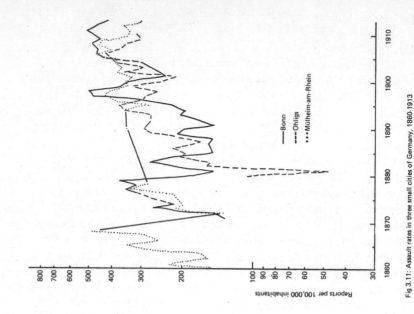

Fig 3.11: Assault rates in three small cities of Germany, 1860-1913

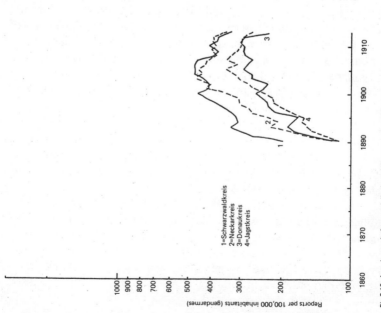

Fig 3.10: Assault rates in four rural districts of Württemberg, 1890-1913

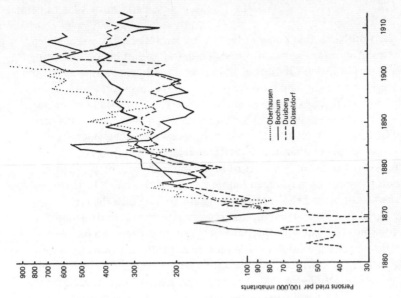

Persons tried per 100,000 inhabitants

Oberhausen
Bochum
Duisberg
Düsseldorf

Fig 3.13: Assault rates in four new industrial cities of Germany, 1863-1913

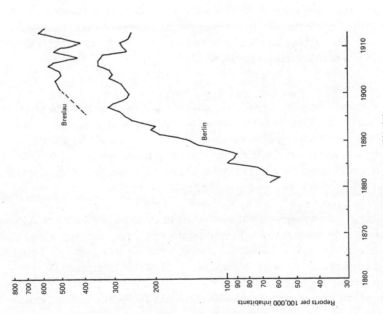

Breslau

Berlin

Reports per 100,000 inhabitants

Fig 3.12: Assault rates in two old cities in Germany, 1881-1913

ment problems that could at first have been reflected in rising violence rates. And since the two or three decades after unification constituted a period of massive industrial and urban growth whose impact was felt everywhere, including rural areas, the fact that even the most rural areas of Württemberg experienced similar patterns is not totally surprising.

Time-series analysis, in short, does suggest a connection between violence and urban growth or perhaps social change in general, but not in any simple or enduring sense. Most evidence seems to point to periods of transition as times of unusually high rates of assault and battery, but this may depend upon specific situations. The nature of the transition and the type of immigrant coming into the city may make a difference. How the community attempts – or does not attempt – to deal with the transition also may affect the pattern; a tight housing situation, for instance, in a rapidly growing city is more conducive to violence than a situation where housing is plentiful and uncrowded. Violence rose, it can be suggested, during times of transition, then fell as adjustments were made, but the exact pattern depended upon the specific situation.

That the conventional wisdom linking violence and the city is false can be posited with more certainty; there is simply no evidence at all that assault rates were higher in cities than in the countryside. Many rural areas had assault rates higher than those in cities, in spite of the fact that rural rates of violence were probably underestimated by official crime records. In the long run, traditions of violence appear to have been a more important determinant of assault rates than either the degree of urbanisation or city size.

Homicide

Contrasts between nineteenth-century patterns of assault and those of homicide are marked. The overall incidence of violence, for instance, may have been higher in Germany than in France, but its severity was greater in France. While assault rates were much greater in Germany, homicide rates were less than half those in France; during the decade 1900-9, 1.76 persons were tried per 100,000 adults for homicide in France as opposed to only 0.76 in Germany.[33] Some of this difference can be accounted for by the inclusion of certain attempted homicides such as poisonings in the French figure, but from what can be discerned about crime categories used in court records, this would not be a large enough number to account for all of the difference. The difference, in short, is probably real.

Over the long run, homicide rates declined slightly in France; rates of persons tried dropped 9 per cent between the 1830s and the 1900s, while rates of cases reported dropped 25 per cent. A graph of annual rates, however, shows that trends differed considerably during the two halves of the century (Fig. 3.14). Rates dropped steadily prior to 1870. They rose around 1870, then began to drop again but at a slower rate. During the last decade of the period they again rose markedly, but whether these latter years marked the beginning of a new trend or simply an unusual cycle in homicide cannot be determined. Trends in homicide, then, were almost the inverse of those in assault in France. Homicides not only dropped while assault rates rose, but the period of greatest decline in homicide rates coincided with the period of highest growth rates in assault.

Homicide rates also dropped steadily in Germany after 1882, but much more drastically than in France during the same period (Fig. 3.15). As in France, they bottomed during the first years of the twentieth century, then moved upward slightly in what may have been the beginning of a new trend. Again, therefore, the incidence of homicides was almost the inverse of that in assaults.

At first glance, the pattern prior to 1882 was different; homicide rates rose somewhat in both Bavaria prior to 1860 and in Prussia between 1854 and 1878. Bavarian statistics, however, include all crimes against life and thus are somewhat unreliable here. And a closer look at the Prussian index shows that rates declined throughout most of the period but started a steep upward climb after a low trough in 1871. Serious assault followed a similar pattern while assault rates as a whole rose during most of the period.

Thus the nature of violence changed in both Germany and France during the nineteenth century: violence became more frequent but possibly less severe. The reasons for this change are difficult to discern. Improved medical facilities may have kept more assault victims alive, thus causing fewer assaults to be classified as homicides, but this factor must have been at least partially offset by the greater availability and effectiveness of lethal weapons such as guns by the end of the period.[34] Larger and more effective police forces may have deterred some serious crimes. Since a high percentage of homicides typically involves family members or close acquaintances, improved family relationships — due to a declining birth rate as well as rising prosperity — may have caused a reduction in homicides.

All of this suggests, in fact, the possibility of an inverse connection between urbanisation and homicide. While contrary to usual assumptions about violence and the city, such a relationship would not be

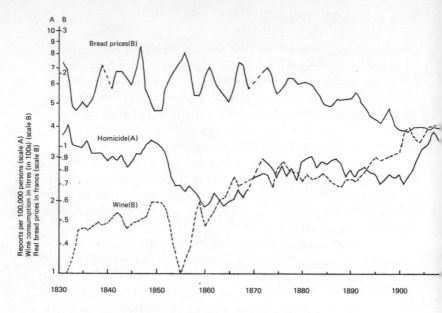

Fig 3.14: Homicide rates, *per capita* wine consumption and real bread prices in France, 1831-1910

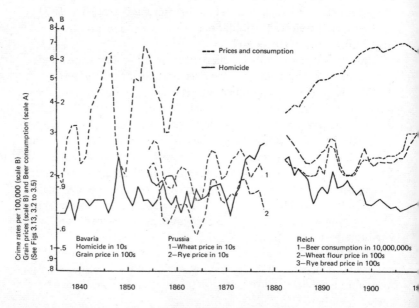

Fig 3.15: Homicide rates, food prices and beer consumption in Germany, 1835-1912

totally illogical. One only need remember the importance of homicidal feuds in many rural settings. City life usually broke up feuds; in the long run, urbanisation may have resulted in improved family relationships, while urban police forces not only deterred feuds but provided an alternate source of punishment to a private village vendetta. For this and other reasons, therefore, a negative relationship between urbanism and homicide proves reasonable, as the facts themselves demonstrate.

Cross-sectional correlations of regional homicide rates and levels of urbanism in Germany and France give conflicting results; the correlation was negative for Germany but positive for France. In both cases, however, the correlation was so low as to be insignificant ($r= -0.13$ and $+0.20$ respectively). These correlations cannot be considered terribly conclusive due to the small numbers involved. Nevertheless, there is no indication here of any link at all between homicide and urban life.

No connection between trends in homicide and the process of urbanisation is apparent either. Correlations between measures of change and levels of homicide in French departments and in German *Regierungs-Bezirke* were insignificant. Likewise, trends in homicide in the areas selected as case studies seem to have had no relationship to urban and industrial growth. As in France as a whole, homicide rates in most of the eight selected French departments dropped significantly prior to 1870; only Bouches-du-Rhône, which lived up to its reputation for violence by having the highest assault rates, experienced rising homicide rates during the first half of the century (Table 3.7). After 1870 homicide rates continued to drop or remained relatively stable in three departments but rose elsewhere. Again, no pattern seems apparent; homicide rates rose in the Nord but fell in Pas-de-Calais; rates also rose in the rural departments of Creuse and Loir-et-Cher, but fell in rural Vendée. Taking the century as a whole, homicide rates dropped or remained relatively stable everywhere except in Bouches-du-Rhône. Similarly, the selected German cities show no apparent groupings on the basis of homicide rates or their trends, though it must be emphasised again that the numbers involved in some cases are minuscule (Table 3.8).

The high homicide rate in Bouches-du-Rhône, which contained Marseilles with its long-standing reputation for violence, suggests that traditions of violence may in fact have been a much more important determinant of homicide rates. A tradition of violence is of course difficult to quantify. However, the highest homicide rate in France (20.98 persons tried per 100,000) occurred, as might be expected, in Corsica, another area with a reputation for violence. And a very high correlation obtained between homicide rates at the beginning and at the end of the period; 66 per cent of the variance in homicide rates in 1900-4 can be explained simply on the basis of rates during the 1830s.

Table 3.7: Homicide Rates in Eight Departments of France During the Nineteenth Century

Departments	Average rates[a]				Percentage change		
	1837-1841	1865-1869	1872-1876	1900-1904	1837/41-1965/69	1872/76-1900/04	1837/41-1900/04
Seine	2.58	1.34	1.66	2.01	−48	+21	−22
Bouches-du Rhône	2.37	3.54	3.67	6.27	+49	+71	+165
Nord	0.92	0.59	0.85	0.98	−36	+15	+ 7
Pas-de-Calais	1.06	0.64	1.05	0.99	−40	− 6	− 7
Loire	2.48	1.00	1.54	1.48	−60	− 4	−40
Vendée	1.94	0.75	0.69	0.32	−61	−54	−84
Loir-et Cher	2.02	1.97	0.37	0.87	− 2	+135	−57
Creuse	1.73	0.50	0.58	0.79	−71	+36	−54

[a]Persons tried per 100,000 inhabitants.

Table 3.8: Homicide rates in nine German cities

City	Average rates[a]		Percentage change
	1881-85	1905-09	1881/85−1905/09
Berlin[b]	0.49	2.75	+461
Chemnitz	?	2.10	−
Düsseldorf	4.09	1.11	− 73
Duisberg	?	3.90	−
Bochum	0	4.97	+497
Oberhausen	3.75	?	−
Bonn	2.39	1.90	− 21
Ohligs	?	4.77	−
Mülheim-am-Rhein	0	4.22	+422

[a]Per 100,000 inhabitants. Exact periods vary slightly.
[b]Some classification problems here.

    Traditions of violence, then, were better predictors of homicide rates than any other variable measured here. Community size or growth, it has been shown, were not at all important. Nor did the proportion of young people strongly affect homicide rates (r=0.21). Alcohol consumption correlated cross-sectionally less strongly with homicide than with theft or even assault; only 8 per cent of the variance in homicide can be explained by alcohol consumption, a result which is surprising in view of the fact that homicide is the crime most frequently assumed to be connected with drinking.[35]

It is interesting to note here that levels of homicide and of assault were relatively independent of one another. Cross-sectional correlations between the two indexes in both Germany and France were positive but not terribly high; the coefficient of correlation was r=0.58 for France and only r=0.34 for Germany. Thus to some extent areas with high rates of total violence tended to have high rates of serious violence and vice versa, but the connection was not close.

Similarly, national time-series suggest some correspondence between peaks and troughs in assault and homicide, but again the correlation was limited. In France, the correspondence was most notable in the 1840s and again possibly after 1900 (see Figs. 3.1 and 3.14). The behaviour of the two indexes in fact was almost identical between 1845 and 1855 except that homicides peaked in 1849, a year before asaults. Both indexes also rose at the end of the century, although the rise in homicide began first. In Germany too, the correlation was mainly limited to a few large cycles (see Figs. 3.2 to 4 and 3.15). In Bavaria the behaviour of the two indexes was quite similar after 1845 and especially between 1845 and 1853, but the correlation was less strong before this time. Similarly, graphs of assault and homicide in Prussia are quite similar after about 1868 but not before. There is scant indication of any correlation in the Reich after 1882.

Little evidence exists to relate homicide rates and prices in either Germany or France, aside from the 'forties and 'fifties when homicide followed the same pattern as assaults (Figs. 3.14 and 3.15). What little evidence there is suggests a positive connection between prosperity and homicide, but the correlation in general is much weaker than for assaults.

Interestingly, however, while the correlation between prices and homicides was fairly weak, the connection between economic conditions and the ratio or balance of the two major forms of lethal violence — homicide and suicide — was stronger.[36] During the early period in France, homicides showed some tendency to rise relative to suicides when prices were low, and to fall relative to suicides during years of high prices (Fig. 3.16). Fluctuations in the mix of these phenomena also corresponded fairly well with those in wine consumption during this time.[37] Thus, although the correlation should not be overemphasised, lethal violence tended to be directed toward the self more often during times of crisis but toward others during periods when prices were low and alcohol consumption high.

But this was only true during the first part of the century. The connection weakened after about 1860 and, while evidences of a correlation between prices and the mix of violent crimes can still be seen. the relationship was much less consistent. Again, however, this loosening might be blamed on the inadequacy of economic indexes which fail to reflect changing standards of living and consumption.

As the preceding discussion suggests, the behaviour of homicide rates was markedly different from that of assault and battery during the nineteenth century. Some instances of similarity can be identified, but in general homicide rates moved quite independently.[38] Nothing suggests that one type of violence served to displace or substitute for the other, but neither can the two indexes be viewed simply as identical aspects of the same phenomenon. Above all, the relationship of the two kinds of violence to urbanisation showed no similarity, a conclusion of vital importance in assessing the impact of the modernisation process on traditional society.

The Theft-Violence Ratio

The relative frequency of violence as compared to property crimes is a dimension of delinquency which is often overlooked. Nevertheless, it is important and can serve to sum up many of our findings about the evolution of crime. How, for instance, does the mix of crimes react to social change or to cycles of crisis and prosperity? Does one type of crime tend to be more important relative to the other in a city than in the countryside; can urban and rural patterns in the composition of crime be identified? Answers to such questions are of course implicit in the preceeding discussion of nineteenth-century crime rates but they still need to be drawn together.

The best way to accomplish this is through the use of a simple theft-violence ratio (TVR = 100 x (homicide + assault)/(homicide + assault + theft)) which measures the composition of crime with a single index. Homicide and assault are totalled here to provide an index of total violence, and theft rates serve as an index of property crimes. The ratio of these two basic indexes indicates the percentage of all three categories which is represented by violence. A ratio below 50, for example, would indicate less than half of all cimes of homicide, assault and theft were were crimes of violence. Similarly, a rising TVR indicates an increasing preference for violence relative to theft.

Such a ratio has several conceptual advantages. It allows the balance between crimes in various areas and times to be compared using a single

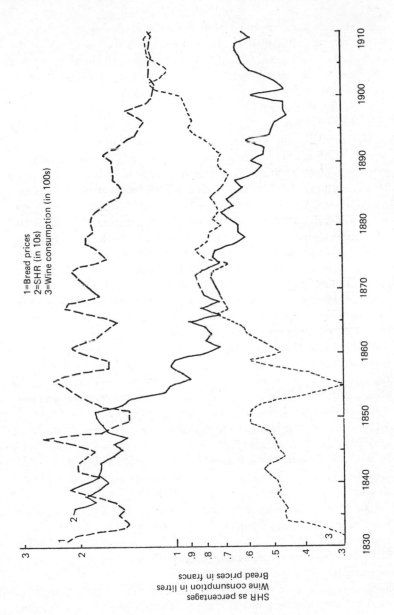

1=Bread prices
2=SHR (in 10s)
3=Wine consumption (in 100s)

Fig 3.16: Annual suicide-homicide ratio, *per capita* wine consumption and real bread prices in France, 1831-1910

index. In fact, cross-sectional comparisons of theft-violence ratios can be made more confidently than can cross-sectional comparisons of the individual crime indexes which make up the ratio. In the theft-violence ratio, indexes of violence in any given area are being compared to indexes of property crime in the same area and therefore distortions due to differing systems of law enforcement and justice are reduced. Here is a case, perhaps of a chain which is stronger than its weakest link.

But, like all good things, the ratio is not without problems. Court records must be used in many cases but, as noted previously, theft rates were increasingly underestimated by such records during the nineteenth century. The slope of trends in a TVR based on court records, therefore, will be too positive, especially after 1870 and in urbanising areas. Similarly, urban-rural biases in both violence and theft cause the TVR to be underestimated in rural or small-town areas as compared to urban. Nevertheless, when these biases are kept in mind, the TVR provides a useful index of the composition of crime.

About half of all persons tried for violence or theft were tried for crimes of violence in both Germany and France at the beginning of the twentieth century, but the ratio was somewhat higher in Germany (52.6) than in France (45.2). Both figures, however, overestimate the TVR due to the high proportion of thefts which were overlooked by court records; using statistics of cases reported in France, for instance, the ratio was 28.4. On the basis of report records, the French ratio fell significantly during the nineteenth century, with most of the decrease coming before 1860; the ratio was relatively steady thereafter (Fig. 3.17). Officially the ratio rose in the Reich after 1882 and in Prussia during the previous decades (Fig. 3.18), but this rise was almost certainly due in part to the decreasing visibility of thefts noted earlier. Both Germany and France thus probably experienced a growing emphsis upon property crimes, or at least theft, in the long run.

The previous discussions of violence and of theft suggest the possibility of urban-rural differentials in the balance or mix of crimes. An examination of the TVR cross-sectionally in France confirms this. The highest correlations in the French cross-sectional analysis were with measures of urbanism, especially the proportion of the population living in large cities.[39] The correlation here was r= −0.59, indicating that the TVR was negatively related to large urbanism and that 35 per cent of the variance in the TVR can be explained by this factor alone, in spite of a bias which would tend to depreciate urban-rural differences.[40] Similarly, in departments with above average levels of large urbanism the average TVR was about 20 per cent lower than in departments of

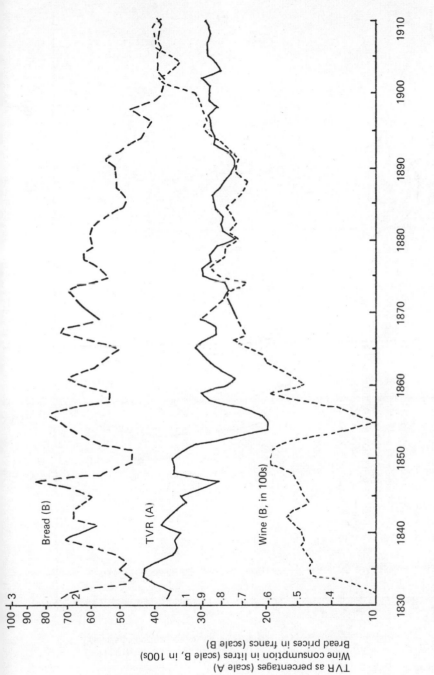

Fig 3.17: Annual theft-violence ratio, *per capita* wine consumption and real bread prices in France, 1831-1910

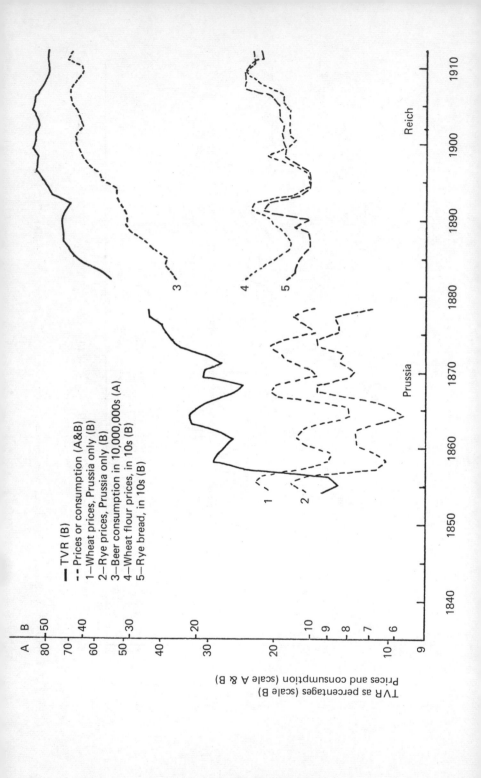

TVR as percentages (scale B)
Prices and consumption (scale A & B)

— TVR (B)
– – Prices or consumption (A&B)
1—Wheat prices, Prussia only (B)
2—Rye prices, Prussia only (B)
3—Beer consumption in 10,000,000s (A)
4—Wheat flour prices, in 10s (B)
5—Rye bread, in 10s (B)

below average percentages of the population living in large cities. In France, then, urban areas tended to have higher levels of theft relative to violence than did rural areas.

Cross-sectional correlations of persons tried in German *Regierungs-Bezirke* give no significant results, but possible deficiencies in these indexes have already been noted. A comparison of major *Stadtkreise* with *Landkreise* and smaller *Stadtkreise* shows a clear correlation: in the 40 *Regierungs-Bezirke* which contained large cities in 1883-7, the average TVR in the 55 major *Stadtkreise* was 28 as opposed to an average of 39 in the 39 *Land-* and small *Stadtkreise*. These results are not due to a skewed distribution or to differences in the administration of justice from *Regierungs-Bezirke* to *Regierungs-Bezirke*; in only one of the *Regierungs-Bezirke* was the TVR in *Landkreise* or small *Stadtkreise* lower than the TVR in the major *Stadtkreise* of the same *Bezirk*.[41]

In both Germany and France, then, large cities manifested a greater incidence of theft compared to violence than did small-town or rural areas. A closer look at regional ratios, however, shows that this correlation was not linear. In Fig. 3.19, three groupings may be seen. Highest theft-violence ratios were all found in very rural departments, while all of the highly urbanised departments had extremely low TVRs. Departments with moderate levels of large city populations, however, were grouped together with more rural departments toward the middle of the scale. While some negative correlation between TVR and substantial urbanism is apparent within this third group, the tendency is not as apparent as in the case of the most rural and most urban departments.[42] Likewise among the cities and regions selected as case studies in Germany and France, TVRs in old urban centres such as Berlin, Paris (Seine) and Marseilles (Bouches-du-Rhône), Chemnitz and Breslau were the lowest in the groups but middle-sized towns or urbanising-industrialising areas often had TVRs as high or higher than rural areas (Tables 3.9 and 3.10). Evidently, then, it was large and/or old urban centres which, with extremely low theft-violence ratios, formed a distinctive group; while there is some evidence that the most rural areas also formed a grouping on the other end of the scale, the distinction here is less clear.

What all this suggests is the existence of a modern pattern of crime, where violence is relatively low compared to property crimes, and a 'pre-modern' pattern of high levels of violence relative to property crimes. Areas in the process of rapid change manifested patterns more similar to pre-modern or rural than modern areas due either to the persistence of rural patterns of crime during the early stages of modern-isation or — and this is not necessarily contradictory — to the tensions of change itself. In urbanising areas, therefore, the *TVR* would be expected to fall only after large-scale urban life was no longer novel.

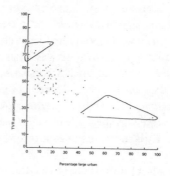

Table 3.9: Average Theft-Violence Ratios in Eight French Departments 1900-4

	TVR
Seine	24.4
Bouches-du-Rhône	31.5
Nord	56.1
Pas-de-Calais	44.8
Loire	39.8
Vendée	52.4
Loir-et-Cher	44.9
Creuse	67.2

Table 3.10: Average Theft-Violence Ratio in 12 German Cities or Districts 1905-9

	TVR
Berlin	15.4
Breslau	18.3
Chemnitz	5.0
Duisberg	25.2
Bochum	29.6
Ohligs	47.9
Mülheim-am-Rhein	30.8
Bonn	28.6
Neckarkreis[a]	35.4
Schwarzwaldkreis	35.3
Donaukreis	26.3
Jagstkreis	27.1

[a]Without Stuttgart

Trends in the theft-violence ratio in the thirteen selected German areas generally were consistent with this periodisation (Figs. 3.20 to 3.23). In most cases, the TVR did drop toward the end of the century as society became more modern. Often, however, the TVR also rose initially, reflecting the rise in violence during the early or most disruptive stages of modern urban and industrial growth. And in general exceptions to this pattern are consistent with the hypothesis; as would be expected, for example, the pattern is less apparent in two quite rural districts of Württemberg and in one or two of the small towns. Only in Bochum do trends not appear to meet expectations.

The situation was less clear in the eight French departments where dependence upon court records causes an upward bias in trends (Figs. 3.24 to 3.27). As would be expected, the TVR was lowest by the end of the period in the two traditionally-urban departments. In the Seine, which had the lowest ratio of the two, the TVR remained relatively steady during the century. In Bouches-du-Rhône the TVR fell rapidly prior to 1870 but rose slightly or, if the trend is biased as expected, remained rather constant thereafter. In the Loire the pattern was similar but somewhat less pronounced. Trends in the two newly industrialising departments were remarkably similar to one another but differed markedly from those in traditional urban-industrial centres. Here the ratio fell at first, rose rapidly during the early years of industrial development, then levelled off or possibly fell after 1870. No significant differences in timing are apparent even though large-scale industrialisation did begin earlier in the Nord than in Pas-de-Calais, but otherwise patterns in these five departments hold about as expected. Only in the three rural departments are movements in the TVR difficult to reconcile with the hypothesis. Overall trend patterns here shared some similarity with trends in the newly industrialising departments. However, the trend after 1870 was more positive in at least two of these rural departments than in the newly industrialising areas indicating, perhaps, the persistence of a traditional pattern of crime, while the rise during the 'fifties and 'sixties might be explained by the large population growth in these rural departments prior to 1870.

The cyclical movement of the TVR is largely predictable from patterns of violence and theft individually: violence was high relative to theft when prices were low and alcohol consumption high but dropped relative to theft during periods of hardship (see Figs. 3.17 and 3.18). And the same periodisation holds true which prevailed for theft by itself. Prior to 1870 the correlation was excellent; the correlation between the TVR and wheat prices in France, for instance, was r= -0.85

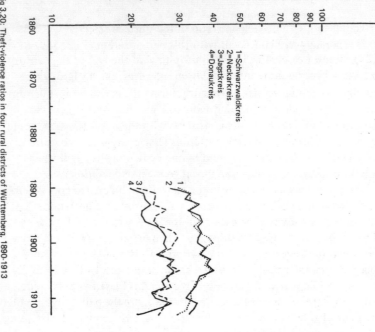

TVR as percentages (gendarmes)

1=Schwarzwaldkreis
2=Neckarkreis
3=Jagstkreis
4=Donaukreis

Fig 3.20: Theft-violence ratios in four rural districts of Württemberg, 1890-1913

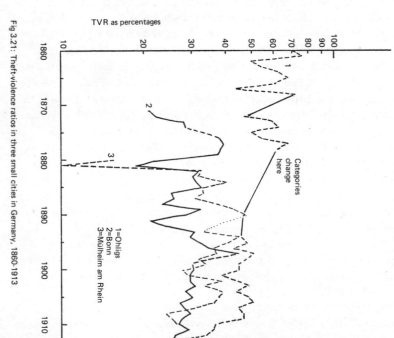

TVR as percentages

Categories
change
here

1=Ohligs
2=Bonn
3=Mülheim am Rhein

Fig 3.21: Theft-violence ratios in three small cities in Germany, 1860-1913

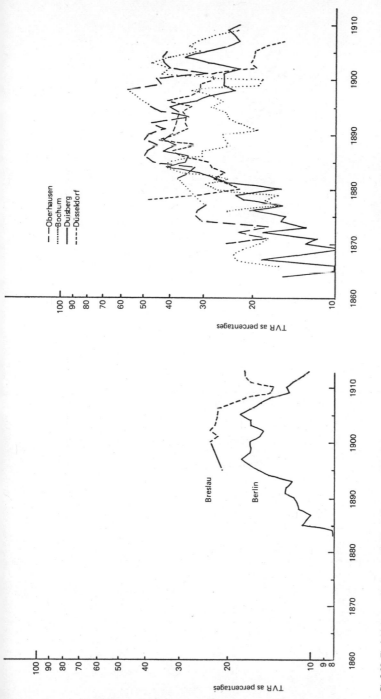

Fig 3.22: Theft-biolence ratios in two old cities in Germany, 1883-1913

Fig 3.23: Theft-violence ratios in four new industrial cities in Germany, 1863-1911

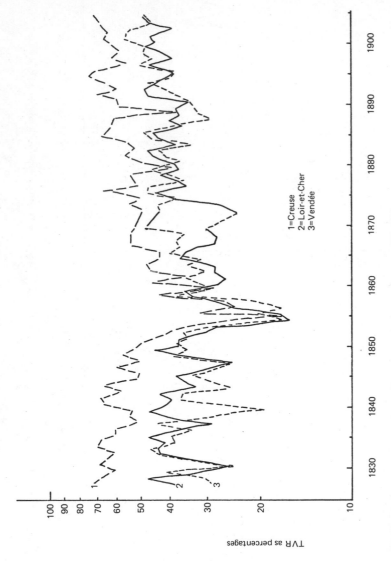

TVR as percentages

1=Creuse
2=Loir-et-Cher
3=Vendée

Fig 3.24: Annual theft-violence ratios in three rural departments of France, 1827-1904

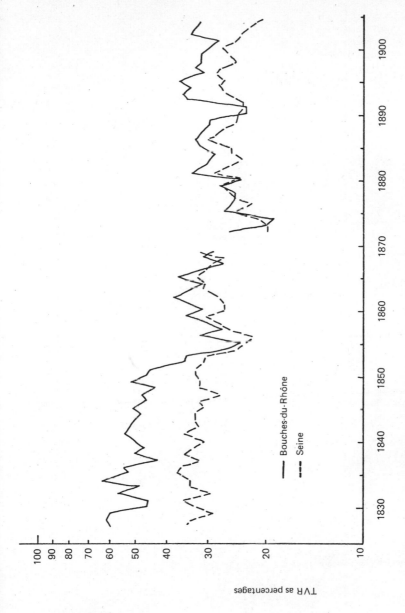

Fig 3.25: Theft-violence ratios in two traditional urban centres in France, 1827-1910

Legend:
——— Bouches-du-Rhône
– – – Seine

TVR as percentages

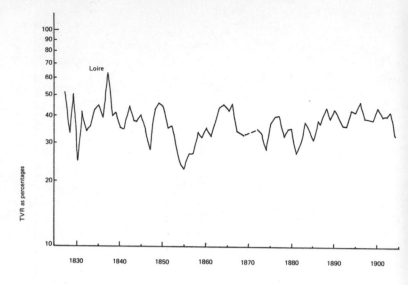

Fig 3.26: Theft-violence ratios in a traditional industrial department of France, 1827-1904

Fig 3.27: Theft-violence ratios in two new urban-industrial departments of France, 1827-1904

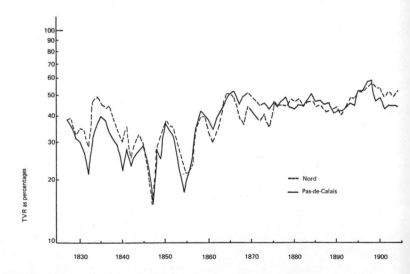

during this period. The 1870s or 1880s again appear to have been a turning point but, at least in France, perhaps less drastically so than was true for either violence or theft individually; although less close, the correlation seems to have continued for several decades after 1870. Nevertheless, evidence again seems to point to a modern and a pre-modern pattern in the cyclical movement of crime.

Conclusion

A complex web of patterns has emerged from this discussion. If nothing else, the impossibility of encompassing the many faces of violence within any single statement or index should be well documented. Nevertheless, some conclusions of a general nature are possible, the most interesting of which are as follows:

1. In general, violence became more frequent but less serious during the course of the nineteenth century. However, a major element of this pattern began to change at the end of the period as rates of violence began to move downward.

2. Contrary to usual assumptions, interpersonal violence was not higher in cities than in the countryside although the initial or most disruptive stages or urban and industrial growth may have caused it to increase.[43]

3. In the long run, tradition remained one of the most important determinants of patterns of violence at the end of the century.

4. Modern and pre-modern patterns in the overall composition of crime seem to have obtained. Violence was low in relation to theft in old, established urban-industrial centres but quite high in relation to theft in rural areas. New urban-industrial areas experienced patterns more similar to rural than to established urban-industrial centres; theft rates rose in these situations, but so did violence.

5. Total violence was negatively related to theft and positively related to the business cycle during the first half of the period.[44] After about 1870 or 1880, however, the relationship may have loosened.

6. Alcohol consumption was positively associated with violence both longitudinally and horizontally, but alcohol consumption was not sufficient to explain the connection between violence and the business cycle.

7. During the first half of the period, homicide rose relative to suicide in times of prosperity and high alcohol consumption but dropped relatively in times of crisis.

Common assumptions about the nature of urban life, these conclusions emphasise once again, are simply wrong; violence is not necessarily peculiarly associated with the city. Nevertheless, the possibility does remain that urban and industrial growth — or at least the most novel and/or disruptive stages of that process — led to violence. But this does not vindicate the social disorganisation hypothesis. Urban growth, it must be stressed once more, does not lead to social disorganisation. But even if it did, such disorganisation would not necessarily lead to violence. In fact, it will be argued here that increases in violence during urban growth represent the retention of traditional patterns of behaviour in the new setting.

In recent years the traditional idyllic picture of rural society has been seriously shaken; it is now widely recognised that social tensions are much higher in rural societies than previously assumed. High rates of violence in the countryside during the nineteenth century indicate that violence — in the form of tavern brawls, family squabbles, even homicidal feuds — was a traditional means of dealing with these tensions. Interpersonal violence, in other words, was a traditional outlet for frustration, an expression of social conflict. In fact, interpersonal violence was often recognised and tolerated as such by villagers and authorities, causing many crimes of violence to be overlooked and thus omitted from crime records in rural areas.

While the view that urbanisation brings social disorganisation must be rejected, urbanisation and industrialisation do create conflicts and frustrations. In such a situation, violence again was a means of dealing with these tensions, especially since other avenues such as collective action were impractical. Thus violence rose as a traditional response to new conflicts and pressures, implying the retention of customary modes of behaviour in the new setting, not complete disorientation and disorganisation. Furthermore, a high percentage of violence has been found to occur between relatives or acquaintances; in the words of Andrew Henry and James Short, homicide — and, implicitly, interpersonal violence in general — is positively correlated with the strength of the relationship system.[45] In the present day, at least, violence is to a large extent predicated upon primary relationships. While this can only tentatively be applied to the nineteenth century, it can be suggested that high rates of violence in urbanising areas attest to the lack of social disorganisation and impersonality in such areas.

All available evidence points to a decline in violence, particularly serious violence, after adjustments to urban and industrial growth. Several alternate explanations for this pattern may be suggested. Violence is intolerable in an urban situation and thus is strongly reproved and repressed. Thus other methods of dealing with conflict and frustration must be worked out; these ways include theft (and possibly suicide) but also some other avenues such as collective action which had not been practical previously but now become conceivable. The decline in violence, in other words, may reflect an acclimatisation to city life, a victory for urban values and social organisation. On the other hand, however, violence may begin to fall off because tensions and conflicts are reduced as adjustments to urbanism and urban growth are made or family relations are improved due to higher standards of living.

This explanation for urban-rural differentials in violence suggests that frustration may be a factor in violence. But at first glance the behaviour of violence through time does not auger well for the relative deprivation/frustration-aggression theory outlined in the introductory chapter. According to this view, relative deprivation leads to frustration, and frustration often results in aggression. But how can relative deprivation and frustration, a form of which has already been used to explain the behaviour of theft, also be used to explain both interpersonal and collective violence, given the differences in the timing of cycles? Moreover, how does one explain the negative relationship between criminal violence and the business cycles during the first half of the century? Why would prosperity increase frustration?

A study of homicide and suicide by Andrew F. Henry and James F. Short, Jr. provides an explanation for these patterns built upon the frustration-aggression concept but making it more specific by employing reference-group theory. Analysing data from the United States, they found patterns very similar to those discovered here. In simplified form, their tentative conclusions were as follows:[46]

1. Much, if not all, aggression is in fact rooted in frustration.

2. But for interpersonal violence, the relevant category of frustration is status frustration, i.e. frustration is defined 'in terms of loss of status position relative to others in the same status reference system'.

3. Homicide was negatively related and suicide positively related to

status, i.e. homicide (and, implicitly, assault and battery) is basically a low status offence while suicide is a high status offence.

4. Social classes or categories of low status lose status relative to high status categories or classes during business expansion while high status categories lose out relative to low status during business contractions. Thus status frustration are greatest for low status, homicide-prone groups during business expansion and homicide or interpersonal violence should be positively related to the business cycle. Conversely, suicide should be negatively related to the business cycle.[47]

In other words, a perceived decline in one's position in relationship to the status of those he compares himself to results in acute frustration, which may lead to violence. During business contraction, it is the upper classes which are hurt most obviously and which lose most in relation to lower-status groups. Thus suicide, which is predominantly a higher-status form of aggression, rises. During periods of prosperity, however, the condition of lower-status groups does not improve as rapidly as that of higher-status groups; lower-status groups, in other words, lose ground relatively (or, in the terminology of relative deprivation theory, status expectations are unfulfilled). A sense of frustration results and interpersonal violence rises as a consequence.

The positive relationship between violence and the business cycle during the first half of the century — a pattern which has been confirmed by a number of studies from other times and places — is thus explainable after all. Why this pattern appears to have dissolved later is unclear, however. One possibility is that new modes of behaviour were adopted; in modern society, perhaps, violence is seen as a less appropriate outlet for frustration, even though the frustrations persist. Perhaps the availability of other outlets such as collective action plus greater prosperity and smoother family relationships reduced the need for interpersonal violence despite frustration. But it is also possible, as was suggested in the discussion of theft, that the indexes of crisis and prosperity used here became less appropriate as expectations and standards of living rose; perhaps, once again, the relationship would be seen to continue if better indicators of business cycles and of status frustration were used.

This interpretation raises several interesting possibilities. Alcohol consumption, it has been maintained, was insufficient to explain the connection between prices and prosperity. The concept of status frustration suggests, rather, that both violence and alcohol consumption were symptoms of the same phenomenon, i.e. of frustrations due to loss of status. Secondly, this interpretation suggests an interesting explanation for the positive correlation between violence and urban growth. Henry and Short found a similar correlation, but concluded that it was an anomaly caused by such factors as the operation of organised crime in disorganised areas.[48] The status frustration theory, however, may be particularly applicable among low-status groups during the early stages of urban and industrial growth. Evidence for this possibility is mixed. For many groups, certainly, urban life and new industrial jobs meant an increase in status. But many were disappointed; the conditions of urban living (e.g. housing) were demeaning, jobs were hard and often did not live up to expectations. The ownership of tangible property, considered so important in rural life, was given up in the city or prior to the move. Low-status groups therefore felt themselves to be losing status during the early years of urban-industrial growth and, once again, the resultant frustrations were expressed through violence. Later, as values and conditions changed, frustrations dropped. Along with the other factors in maturing cities, this made violence no longer so necessary or appropriate as earlier.

These interpretations are inherently quite speculative. Macro-analysis, though in many ways a precondition for any closer study, is not adequate to deal with such issues with any degree of precision. Distinctions need to be made between the criminal behaviour of various social classes, age and marital groups, and different sectors of cities, to cite just a few cases. Nevertheless, these interpretations do generally fit the patterns of violence observed in Germany and France during the nineteenth century and they do provide reasonable explanations for patterns that are otherwise quite surprising.

4 CONCLUSION

What then happened to crime during the nineteenth century? Can any general statement be made about patterns in crime during this period? By now the pitfalls in such a question are obvious. Statements about crime-in-general are often misleading because of substantial differences in the behaviour of various crime categories — although it is noteworthy that each crime category appears to have had its own characteristic pattern of behaviour which, in many cases, transcended regional or national boundaries. Similarly, the tenuous nature of many national averages and patterns of crime is clear; regional patterns or styles of crime obtained which often were rather independent of national boundaries. Nevertheless, the question is legitimate and several conclusions about nineteenth-century criminal behaviour are indeed possible.

The most important general phenomenon which has been observed here was the change in the nature of criminal behaviour which took place during the century, especially in non-rural areas. The dimensions of this change were several. Crime rates in general, but especially property crime rates, rose during the nineteenth century; on the whole, then, crime was more frequent by 1913 than it had been in 1830. Against this must be balanced, however, the declining importance of violence — and especially serious violence — relative to theft in the long run. Concurrently, a change occurred in the economic determinants of crime: the relationship between basic subsistence costs and both violent and property crimes loosened as the century progressed due, seemingly, to rising standards of living. But neither of these developments occurred instantly. A transitional stage has been observed in which violence kept up with or even outstripped rising theft rates while the connection between crime and costs of basic staples loosened only gradually.

This transitional period, during which crime rates soared particularly rapidly, had a potential impact well beyond its own duration. The rapid rise in crime occurred as many social groups, including the new middle class, were being exposed to city life for the first time. It could give an empirical base to a sense that urban life was dangerous, even out of hand, and thus strengthen such important new trends as residential segregation, and ultimately suburbanisation, by class. And the resultant fear of the city could outlive the actual transitional period of crime itself. It has certainly stimulated impressions of a relationship between

city and crime not only in the public mind but also among many
scholarly analysts of crime as well.

But the long-term evolution in patterns of criminal behaviour, which
includes a more modest tendency toward an increase in crime rates, is
more significant in actuality. This alteration in patterns of criminal
behaviour has been characterised here as a transition from pre-modern
to modern forms of criminal behaviour, reflecting the eventual aban-
donment of rural traditions, rising standards of living and thus rising
expectations, and in general adjustment to life in an urban, industrial
society. What we have traced, in other words, is a modernisation of
criminal behaviour paralleling and accompanying the modernisation
of society in general. But a word of caution is in order. This investigation has stopped at the First World War, and thus cannot tell us whether
the pre-war patterns which we have termed modern have in fact persisted since then. A spot check suggests that they may have — according
to French correctional court records, for example, the TVR in France
continued its decline after the war so that in 1941-50 it was only
0.17, or less than half the level of a century earlier; but changes in the
administration of justice since the First World War make comparisons
between pre-war and present patterns difficult.[1]

Data from the United States in the twentieth century are interesting
in the context of this problem. Overall, the pattern here seems similar
to that seen for Germany and France in the nineteenth century; violence is low relative to theft (TVR= 0.05 for the period 1960-73, with
no apparent trend during these years) and, at least in the early 1950s,
the TVR was significantly higher in rural areas (0.08) than in urban
areas (0.04). But a closer examination of some U.S. statistics indicates
an important difference (Table 4.1).[2]

Table 4.1: Theft-Violence Ratios in Urban and Rural Areas of the United
States, 1966-7. Population Size Classes in Thousands

All cities	.048
1.000+	.088
500–1,000	.053
250–500	.045
All, 250+	.060
100–250	.046
50–100	.034
25–50	.034
10–25	.050
under 10	.041
Suburbs	.037
Rural Areas	.071

The expected urban-rural difference in the theft-violence ratio did hold true generally in 1966-7; the average TVR was significantly higher in the rural group than in the urban group. But unlike the nineteenth-century European pattern, violence rates in the very largest cities in the nation were much higher relative to theft than anywhere else, including rural areas, while the TVR in most small-town groups was significantly lower than in either the most urban or the most rural areas. This difference in patterns raises an interesting question: should these differences in criminal behaviour be attributed to national or to chronological differences? That national differences may obtain is reasonable, of course; it is highly likely that crime patterns in a mobile, frontier society would differ from those in a European context. But there are also numerous reasons why patterns may be expected to have changed during the past half century or so, and this would not necessarily be inconsistent with the interpretation which we have advanced here. The great wars of the twentieth century, for example, to some extent upset previous trends and patterns of behaviour. The 'second' industrial revolution based on new sources of energy and a new cluster of technological achievements has brought new disruptions and has forced new adjustments upon European as well as American society. The emergence of the 'post-industrial city' has changed the nature of urban life: with the rise of metropolitan communities and the increasing importance of suburban life, the city has become less centralised; the urban economy has become more service-centred; new patterns of immigration to — as well as emigration from — the city have emerged; and the spread of mass communication has broken down many rural-urban distinctions, resulting in the 'urbanisation' of rural society. Hi-jackings, kidnappings and 'rip-offs' in the 1970s suggest that crime is becoming increasingly politicised. What has been identified here as a modern pattern of crime thus may only be modern in the context of the nineteenth century, describing an intermediate pattern of crime characteristic of a specific historical period. The continuous, open-ended nature of the historical process must, that is, be affirmed.

But is the 'modernisation' of criminal patterns, even if confined to the nineteenth century, applicable beyond the two countries studied? It is premature to speculate too fully without further research, but the congruence of patterns in the two countries might seem persuasive. Thus it is interesting to compare these findings to those of another recent historical study of crime, that by J.J. Tobias, which has related nineteenth-century crime patterns to modernisation in England.

Tobias' results are at variance with those found here for Germany and France at several points. Tobias claims to have discerned an actual long-term decline in crime during the century, for instance, and he found no recurrent connection with fluctuations in economic conditions.[3] His study concerns England rather than the continent and of course it is possible that the English experience was distinctive. At the same time, Tobias' conclusions must be considered exceedingly tentative because he often does not distinguish between types of crimes and because, since he opted for literary rather than quantitative sources, his conclusions are necessarily impressionistic. Interestingly, however, at one very important point his findings are consistent with ours. Among juvenile offenders, at least, Tobias found very high and perhaps rising rates of crime in the initial stages of industrialisation but then a decrease after about 1850.[4] As in Germany and France, in other words, a period of substantial urbanisation and industrialisation coincided with a period of high crime rates followed by some stabilisation or even a decline in criminality. The transitional stage in the modernisation of criminality is thus confirmed by his findings.

Tobias' explanations are traditional. High rates during the first half of the century are attributed to the lack of opportunities for 'honest work', to poor educational facilities, to congested housing, to 'the pernicious effects of a morally unhealthy urban environment'. Most important, however, is his emphasis on social disorganisation: urbanisation meant the breakdown of the family, personal disorientation, a cultural shock which naturally led to crime. The eventual stabilisation or decrease in criminality, then, came about because of a 'more settled social environment'. By this time the number of immigrants to the city had fallen off and cities were taking steps to make urban life more pleasant. Also, the improvement of urban police forces, the increased certainty of punishment due to judicial reforms, improvements in education and, finally, the development of reform schools — an interesting argument, given what is known about the effects of reform schools today — all helped to reduce crime.[5]

The inadequacies of this interpretation by now are basically familiar; there is no need to belabor them. However, the Tobias book and its popularity do illustrate the persistence of this sort of outlook, and it does provide a useful contrast to the interpretation outlined here. Crime is not, we argue, a symptom of social and moral disorganisation; the argument stressing these factors would be hard pressed to explain patterns of crime in any but the initial stages of nineteenth-century industrialisation, and even there it is inadequate. Changing patterns of crime do reflect and reveal changing value and social systems, but not

'normlessness' or social disorganisation. Rising theft rates indicate
rising expectations, the spread of 'modern' economic values and, with
some qualification, are characteristic of modern, urban society. In a
sense, therefore, theft represents an adaptation to modern social goals,
although it of course reflects a rejection of – or even a protest against
– socially legitimate means of reaching such goals. Violence, on the
other hand, represents a traditional form of criminal behaviour, and its
rise in a situation of change reflects the retention rather than the breakdown of traditional behaviour. Interpersonal violence is an expression
of frustration and tension, a form of social conflict. To some extent it
might be viewed as a form of primitive, 'unrealistic' protest against
developments in society and the economy. Thus criminal violence
might usefully be seen as an index of social tensions, with drops in violence indicating reductions in tension and, in the long run, the abandon-
ment of traditional forms of behaviour.

Such suggestions must, of course, remain tentative at this point.
Again, quantitative analysis at the national or even the regional level
cannot explore these possibilities with much precision. What are needed
now are closer investigations of specific groups such as urban immigrants
or sections of the working class, case studies of small areas such as new
industrial cities, and qualitative treatments of criminal records and
actual case histories. We need, for instance, to know more about who
offenders actually were and the reasons they gave for having committed
crimes and we need to investigate the differential response of such
social groups to the variables mentioned here. But it is clear, now, what
should be looked for.

For our findings constitute an important if incomplete beginning,
after several impressionistic false starts, for quantitative analysis on the
macro level is in many ways a precondition for such close approaches.
Macro analysis has already told us of the loosening of traditional links
between property crimes and subsistence crises, as well as the growing
concentration on this kind of crime as opposed to violence. The con-
version of individual criminals such as Kürper, the German vagrant-
turned-thief cited in the introduction, based on new material expectations and grievances, can be noted as a first step to the case study
approach which is now needed to flesh out the relationship between
crime and the modernisation of society at large. Indeed, because crime
was normally an individual act, easier to mount than organised protest,
it may have reflected new expectations earlier than the strikes and riots
that have more commonly been the subject of historical attention. The
relationship between banditry and other social unrest has been noted

for groups on the verge of modernisation;[6] the present study confirms
this, in broad outline, for the period in which urban crime was in transition, expressing a new intensity of conflict but in rather traditional
forms. We can add now the possibility that the modernisation of crime,
after this dramatic period, was a vital part of more adaptive social
change. Judging by the larger patterns of crime, modern offenders,
however much they felt left out of modern society, wanted in and saw
crime as a way to realise modern values.

Postscript: Some Implications

This book is an exercise in history, not theory. Nevertheless, the interpretation advanced in the preceding pages, if valid, has some important
implications for the way in which we view   and respond to − crime. I
have noted a number of these already, but several are worth reiteration,
not because they are novel, but because they are important.

Crime, many people assume, is irrational, dysfunctional, even pathological behaviour; it is a disease and just may be symptomatic of the
malignancies of modern and/or urban life. This interpretation, however,
suggests the opposite. In the first place, much crime must be seen as
'rational' in the same sense as is choosing a new job or getting married;
it is a response to a situation or a problem, and is often the result of
decision no more irrational than many other decisions in life. A ghetto
dweller who, when faced with limited options, steals a car in order to
attain what our value system defines as the good life or, on the other
hand, to flaunt and protest against the methods and/or problems of
realising these values is making a decision, often based directly or
indirectly on an evaluation of the alternatives and possible consequences before him. So do we all, and not much more rationally or
irrationally for that matter. Crime, then, is in some sense rational, the
result of a decision and is not categorically different from the behaviour
of 'non-offenders'.

Nor is crime completely or even primarily dysfunctional; indeed,
crime serves a function for both the offender and society. For society,
this interpretation suggests, crime is functional because it serves as a
safety valve, draining off frustrations and anger that might otherwise −
and quite logically − be directed against society's structure and foundations. Ironically, the thief who steals a car to attain the standard of
living which he feels has been promised or in order to rebel against the
society which seemingly has denied him of it may have helped preserve
society in its present form. And the same may be true, this interpretation suggests, for the man who assaults his wife. Moreover, as others

have suggested, crime may serve additional purposes for society or for specific social groups by helping them define their boundaries *vis-à-vis* other societies or groups, and possibly also by helping to counter the tendencies toward stagnation and rigidity which are present in all societies. But crime is also functional for the offender by providing an outlet for frustration, a channel for obtaining a goal, or a means of protesting. This is why crime cannot be seen as merely dysfunctional, purposeless, pathological behaviour.

Finally, we need to realise that crime is inherently political.[7] If crime often does imply a rejection of or a protest against society or its norms, then it is obviously a political act on the part of the offender. But crime is also highly political from the vantage point of society. It is of course often the result of political decisions, such as the decision not to enforce gun laws or to use unemployment as a means of combating inflation. But the political nature of crime goes deeper than that, for crime by its very definition is political; it flows from political decisions as to what acts will be considered 'criminal' and, even more importantly, from decisions as to exactly who will be termed 'criminal'. Crime — its commission, its causes, its definition, its enforcement — is a political act, and not until we admit this fact can we begin to deal with the phenomenon fairly.

By no means am I sympathetic with the conservative position which places the entire responsibility on the offender, denying the environment in which decisions are made. But neither can I accept the old liberal position which assumes a kind of determinism that absolves the individual of all moral responsibility. In fact, my concern here has nothing to do with the question of blame. I am more interested in our learning to understand offenders by realising that their behaviour is not unlike our own, as ongoing participants in a modernising society. In order to confront the problem (and is crime the real problem; or is it the causes which produce crime? Our identification of the essential issue may be obscured by our own fears and prejudices), we will have to eliminate that mystique about crime which helps make it so unfathomable. Only in this way can we ever confront the offender in understanding and compassion and thus begin to make some progress toward resolution.

All of this brings us, of course, back to Durkheim, where we began. Crime is normal; it plays a definite role in society, and it involves behaviour not so dissimilar from that of non-offenders. We can conclude on this point. But as crime and society move in similar directions, we can also ask if it is eternally necessary for society to have crime in order to define itself.

NOTES

Chaper 1

1. This view is discussed in Emile Durkheim, *The Rules of the Sociological Method*, trans. Sarah A. Salovay and John M. Mueller (Glencoe, Ill., 1950), pp. 65-73.

2. Recent studies of white-collar crime demonstrate that crime pervades the entire social structure more thoroughly than is often assumed. See, for instance, the pioneering study by Edwin H. Sutherland, *White-collar Crime* (New York, 1950). Cf. Erik Olin Wright, *The Politics of Punishment: A Criticical Analysis of Prisons in America* (New York, 1973), p. 3.

3. An interesting adaptation and application of this suggestion is represented by Kai Erickson, *Wayward Puritans: A Study in the Sociology of Deviance* (New York, 1966).

4. A.M. Guerry, *Essai sur la statistique morale de la France* (Paris, 1833). A useful bibliography of nineteenth-century material on crime may be found in William A Bonger, *Criminality and Economic Conditions*, trans. Henry P. Horton (New York, 1967), while several more recent surveys may be found in the bibliography at the end of this essay.

5. The nineteenth century is defined here as the period from about 1830 to 1914 for several reasons. This period spans the classic era of industrialisation and urbanisation; large-scale changes did not begin in most areas until at least several decades after Waterloo and, once they did begin, were fairly continuous until the First World War at least. Good criminal statistics also did not begin until at least 1830 − and often later − while certain changes in judicial and recording systems around 1914 interrupt most crime series at that point, making the First World War a useful terminating point. Thus the period forms a viable unit from both a socio-economic and a methodological point of view.

6. See, for instance, J.J. Tobias, *Urban Crime in Victorian England* (New York, 1972), and V.A.C. Gatrell and T.B. Hadden, 'Criminal Statistics and their Interpretation', in *Nineteenth-Century Society: Essays in the Use of Quantitative Methods for the Study of Social Data*, ed. E.A. Wrigley (Cambridge, England, 1972), pp. 336-62.

7. Over half (54 per cent) of the German population lived in cities of 2,000 or more persons by 1900 while France did not become 50 per cent urban until 30 years later. 40 per cent of the economically active population in Germany was employed in industry in 1901-7, as opposed to only 31 per cent in France. Koppel S. Pinson, *Modern Germany and Its History*, 2nd ed. (New York, 1967), pp. 221-2; Georges Dupeux, *La société française 1789-1960* (Paris, 1964), pp. 21-2, 32-3. See also 'Evolution de la population active en France depuis cent ans d'après de dénombrements quinquenaux', *Etudes et Conjectures* (May-June 1953), pp. 230-88, and 'Quelques aspects de évolution des populations actives dans les pays d'Europe occidentale', *ibid.* (November 1954), pp. 971-1012.
A useful discussion of industrialisation generally is David Landes, 'Technological Change and Development in Western Europe, 1750-1914', in *The Cambridge Economic History of Europe*, Vol. VI, Part I (Cambridge, England, 1965), pp. 274-601.

8. A valuable though slightly dated discussion of the FBI's crime figures is provided by Fred. P. Graham, 'A Contemporary History of American Crime',

in Hugh Davis Graham and Ted Robert Gurr (eds.), *Violence in America: Historical and Comparative Perspectives*, (New York, 1969), pp. 460-78. An example of the sceptical view in regard to English statistics is J.J. Tobias, *Urban Crime*, pp. 14-21. But the same statistics are viewed in a more positive light by V.A.C. Gatrell and T.B. Hadden, 'Criminal Statistics', pp. 336-62.

9. A detailed examination of the validity of problems in nineteenth-century crime records is provided in Howard Zehr, 'Patterns of Crime in Nineteenth-Century Germany and France: A Comparative Study' (unpublished Ph.D. dissertation, Rutgers University, 1974), Chapter II. A discussion and catalogue of available crime statistics for the nineteenth century is also provided in Chapter II and the Appendix. Interestingly, the reliability of crime indexes does not appear to have improved greatly during the past century; rates of crimes cleared up, for instance, are strikingly similar for the nineteenth and twentieth centuries. Rising crime levels combined with the increased complexity of crime solution in a more populous urban environment and, perhaps, an increasingly sophisticated group of offenders may have helped offset the numerous advances in forensic science such as fingerprinting, cross-referenced offender files, and so on. Another example of the literature dealing with these problems is Thorsten Sellin and Marvin E. Wolfgang, *The Measurement of Delinquency* (New York, 1964).

10. While the total number of complaints and reports to French police nearly doubled between 1857 and 1900, the number of policemen empowered to receive them increased by only 41 per cent. Whereas in 1857 there was one agent for every 360 persons, in 1900 there was one agent for every 470. Based on crime records in the *Compte général de l'administration de la justice criminelle en France*, 1857, Table XCCIV, pp. 211-28, and 1900, Table XLVI, pp. 106-7.

11. In France, for instance, rates of persons tried for theft rose 60 per cent between 1830-9 and 1900-9 while rates of reports to public prosecutors rose 230 per cent. Indexes of persons tried and of persons convicted in Germany 1882-1912 show a similar divergence. Nevertheless, the correspondence between cyclical movements in the two indexes is quite good. See Appendix A-3. Based on statistics in annual *Compte général* and the *Kriminalstatistik* volumes of the *Statistik des deutschen Reichs* for these years. The index of reports to prosecutors is discussed later in the text. See note 15. It is important to note here that an additional negative bias is introduced if one concentrates, as it is tempting to do given the useful form that these statistics are given in, on serious crimes tried in higher courts. Charles, Louise and Richard Tilly, for example, in their recent *The Rebellious Century, 1830-1930 (Cambridge, Mass., 1975)*, pp. 79-80, find that assize records show a massive *fall* in serious property crimes during the nineteenth century, and thus conclude that the present century is no more disorderly than the previous one. The error here is serious and provides a perfect example of the potential for misinterpretation inherent in crime statistics. Besides the increasing numbers of property crimes which were simply dropped, more and more cases were sent to lower courts during the century; many observers commented (and the statistics suggest that they were right) that prosecutors sent increasing numbers of cases to lower courts in order to speed up the process of justice and to increase the probability of convictions.

12. 'Unofficial' crime statistics which can be gleaned from such diverse sources as insurance records, fire department reports and mortality statistics deserve more attention they have received. However, these statistics do contain some

serious deficiencies.
13. For discussions of weighted indexes see Zehr, 'Patterns of Crime', pp. 138-41, and Sellin and Wolfgang, *Measurement*, pp. 236-318.
14. Published annually in the *Staats-Anzeiger für Württemberg*, 1849 ff.
15. Both components of this index are included in the annual *Compte général*. Cases tried (*accusations* or *affaires*) are listed in separate tables of statistics for assizes and correctional courts. Where appropriate, statistics from these two courts were added together, but to give as complete a picture of cases tried as possible, statistics of cases tried by *contumace*, or default – listed in separate tables – were also included. All cases dropped except those which were found not to have involved an offence were totalled to give total crimes dropped. Thus the index of crimes reported consists of total cases tried plus total cases dropped minus those found not to be crimes. This index is not perfect, of course, but does represent a great improvement over simple court records.
16. A brief but useful abstract of Shaw and McKay's work on delinquency may be found in Ernest W. Burgess and Donald J. Bogue, 'The Delinquency Research of Clifford R. Shaw and Henry D. McKay', in Burgess and Bogue (eds.), *Urban Sociology* (Chicago, 1967), pp. 293-317.
17. The classic work on suicide and anomie is, of course, Emile Durkheim, *Suicide: A Study in Sociology* (New York, 1951). A critique of his approach is provided by Jack D. Douglas, The Social Meanings of Suicide (Princeton, 1967). Elwin H. Powell, 'Crime as a Function of Anomie', *Journal of Criminal Law, Criminology and Police Science*, 57 (June 1966), pp. 161-71, is an example of this anomie theory applied to crime.
18. For a discussion of society's role in defining deviance see Howard S. Becker, *Outsiders: Studies in the Sociology of Deviance* (New York, 1966).
19. Gideon Sjoberg, 'Theory and Research in Urban Sociology', in Philip M. Hauser and Leo F. Schnore (eds.), *The Study of Urbanization* (New York, 1967), pp. 159-68, provides a brief overview of this urban concept. See also Leonard Reissman, *The Urban Process: Cities in Industrial Societies* (Glencoe, Ill., 1964), pp. 23-4, 89-144. The development and pervasiveness of this (as well as the ecological) outlook is surveyed briefly by Don Martindale, 'Prefatory Remarks: The Theory of the City', in Max Weber, *The City*, trans. and ed. Don Martindale and Gertrud Neuwirth (New York, 1966), pp. 9-62.
20. Georg Simmel, 'The Metropolis and Mental Life', in Paul K. Hatt and Albert J. Reiss (eds.), *Reader in Urban Sociology* (Glencoe, Ill., 1951), pp. 563-74; Louis Wirth, 'Urbanism as a Way of Life', *American Journal of Sociology*, 44 (July 1938), pp. 1-24.
21. And a survey of historical literature attests to the importance of such assumptions in this discipline.
22. Critical treatments of this urban theory and of the rural-urban continuum are included in Philip M. Hauser, 'Observations on the Urban-Folk and Urban-Rural Dichotomies as Forms of Western Ethnocentrism', in *The Study of Urbanization*, pp. 503-7, Oscar Lewis, 'Further Observations on the Folk-Urban Continuum and Urbanization with Special Reference to Mexico City', in *ibid.*, pp. 491-503; Sjoberg, 'Theory and Research', in *ibid.*, pp. 158-68; Richard Dewey, 'The Rural-Urban Continuum: Real but Relatively Unimportant', *American Journal of Sociology*, 66 (July 1960), pp. 60-6; Reissman, *The Urban Process*, pp. 131 ff.; Charles T. Stewart, Jr., 'The Urban-Rural Dichotomy: Concepts and Uses', *American Journal of Sociology*, 64 (September 1958), pp. 152-8; and various essays in Paul K. Hatt and Albert J. Reiss, Jr. (eds.), *Cities and Society: The Revised Reader*

in Urban Sociology (New York, 1967).

23. Oscar Lewis, 'Further Observations', and 'The Culture of Poverty', in J.J. TePaske and S.N. Fisher (eds.), *Explosive Forces in Latin America* (Columbus, Ohio, 1964), pp. 149-73. Herbert J. Gans, *The Urban Villagers: Group and Class in the Life of Italian-Americans* (Glencoe, Ill., 1962).

24. Reprinted in Donald R. Cressey and David A. Ward (eds.), *Delinquency, Crime and Social Process* (New York, 1969), pp. 254-84. A reconciliation between this concept of anomie and differential association theory is attempted by Richard A. Cloward in *ibid.*, pp. 312-31. A useful collection of essays on the possible relationship between anomie and crime is Marshall B. Clinard (ed.), *Anomie and Deviant Behavior* (New York, 1964).

25. Ted Robert Gurr, *Why Men Rebel* (Princeton, 1971); and Jamces C. Davies, 'The J-Curve of Rising and Declining Satisfactions as a Cause of Some Great Revolutions and a Contained Rebellion', in Graham and Gurr, *Violence in America*, pp. 671-709.

26. The literature dealing with the frustration-aggression hypothesis is too voluminous to note here. However, a useful bibliography of this material is included in Gurr, *Why Men Rebel*, pp. 369-407.

27. Attempts to apply and test this theory for collective violence include Ted Robert Gurr, 'A Comparative Study of Civil Strife', in Graham and Gurr, *Violence in America*, pp. 544-605, and Ivo K. Feierabend *et al.*, 'Social Change and Political Violence: Cross-National Patterns', in *ibid.*, pp. 606-67.

28. Lewis Coser, *The Functions of Social Conflict* (New York, 1964), p. 40. Cf. Davies, 'The J—Curve', p. 672.

29. Coser, *Social Conflict*, pp. 40-54.

30. This is the central point of Coser's work. See especially *ibid.*, p. 38, for a brief summary of the functions of conflict.

31. *Ibid.*, pp. 48-55.

32. Cf. *ibid.*, p. 51.

33. Quoted in Arthur Griffiths, *German and Austrian Prisons* (London, 1851), pp. 202-3.

34. Eldridge Cleaver, *Post-Prison Writings and Speeches*, ed. Robert Scheer (New York, 1969), p. 157.

35. Gatrell and Hadden, 'Criminal Statistics', pp. 336-8, have recently made a similar suggestion. Interestingly, for examples they have focused on the same issues as the present essay, i.e. the relationship between crime, social tensions and standards of living – but their tentative suggestions are somewhat at odds with our findings.

Chapter 2

1. In order to make the French and the German records as comparable as possible, the category of theft here includes a number of related crimes such as receiving, robbery or burglary which involve the taking of property.

2. A sample of the literature dealing with crime and economic conditions is included in the bibliography. Brief surveys of opinions and studies may be found in Vold, *Theoretical Criminology*, p. 159, and in J. Thorsten Sellin, *Research Memorandum on Crime in the Depression*, Social Science Research Bulletin 27 (New York, 1937). The nineteenth-century debate is reviewed in more detail by Bonger, *Criminality*, pp. 1-246, and, for England, more briefly in Tobias, *Urban Crime*, pp. 150-7.

3. John Clay, 'On the Effect of Good or Bad Times on Committals to Prison', *Journal of the Statistical Society of London*, 18 (March 1855), p. 74.

4. *Statistik der Gerichtlichen Polizei im Königreiche Bayern und in einigen*

anderen Lander, Heft XVI, of *Beiträge zur Statistik des Königreichs Bayern* (Munich, 1867).

5. 'Lebensmittelpreise. Beschäftigungsgrad und Kriminalität', *Archive für Sozialwissenschaft und Sozialpolitik* 61, Heft 3 (Tübingen, 1929), pp. 21-62.

6. French trial statistics are based upon data in the annual *Compte général de l'administration de la justice criminelle en France.* Construction of the index of reports to prosecutors, which is based upon data in the same source, is discussed in the preceding chapter. German statistics 1882-1912 come from the annual *Kriminalstatistik* volumes included in the *Statistik des deutschen Reichs.* Unless otherwise noted, national rates for France are calculated per 100,000 persons 10 years or older, while German rates are per 100,000 non-military persons 12 years or older; where possible, that is, persons under 10 or 12, who presumably commit few crimes and, when they did, would not normally appear in court, have been left out of population figures. Where appropriate, French statistics include trials by assize and correctional courts as well as those decided by *contumace* or default. Similarly, German indexes include both felonies and misdemeanors. The fraud-embezzlement group does not include the many minor infractions such as 'fraud by restaurant operators' which are included in French correctional statistics. For discussion of method of calculating rates, see Appendix A-1.

7. See, for instance, Georg Mayr, *Statistik und Gesellshaftslehre,* Band III, *Moralstatistik* (Tübingen, 1917), pp. 553-4.

8. Rough estimates based on statistics contained in tables of crimes tried and tables of cases dropped in annual *Compte général* around the turn of the century. The person-case ratio is based on the ratio between charges and persons in court records, while the solution rate is based upon the percentage of cases dropped because no offender was identified. Using these figures, the 'corrected' rate of persons tried in France would be (392.80/.70) x 0.60 = 336.69.

9. As noted in Chapter 1, half of the German population lived in cities by 1900 while France did not reach this point until about 1930.

10. Based on the statistics in annual volumes of *Statistisches Jahrbuch für Grossherzogtum Baden,* 1882-1914. Population figures used for calculating rates excluded the eight cities which had their own police forces and reported separately in the *Jahrbuch.* Rates are per 100,000 inhabitants of all ages.

11. Württemberg crime statistics come from the *Staats-Anzeiger*; from F. Zahn, 'Aufgaben und Leistungen der Polizeistatistik', *Allgemeines Statistisches Archiv* IX, Heft 2/3 (Munich, 1915), p. 375; and from 'Königsliches Landjägercorps: Uebersicht über die Festnahmen und Anzeigen', 1900-13, Hauptstaatsarchiv Stuttgart MSS, E151cII No. 429. Rates have been based on the entire population of Württemberg, minus that of the city of Stuttgart which had its own independent criminal police.

12. See preceding note.

13. Bavarian crime statistics come from Mayr, *Statistik der Gerichtlichen Polizei,* appendix, and from *Beiträge zur Statistik des Königreichs Bayern* (Munich, 1853-65). Prussian statistics may be found in W. Starke, *Verbrechen und Verbrecher in Preussen 1854-78* (Berlin, 1884), and in J. Illing, 'Die Zahlen der Kriminalität in Preussen für 1854 bis 1884', in *Zeitschrift des Könglich-Preussischen Statistischen Bureaus* XXV (Berlin, 1885), p.1 ff. The latter statistics include only the eight 'old' provinces of Prussia, i.e. Prussia (East and West), Posen, Pomerania, Silesia, Brandenburg, Saxony, Westphalia, and Rheinland. Schleswig-Holstein, Hanover and Hesse-Nassau are excluded.

14. Or 92 per cent if rates per million buildings rather than inhabitants are used. Based on statistics in the *Württembergische Jahrbucher für Statistik und*

Landeskunde, 1899 (Heft II), pp. 96-7.

15. Eight cities had their own criminal police by the 1880s, though they probably did not all have them in the 1830s. Since rates have been calculated without the population of these cities for both periods, however, rates in the 1830s are probably overestimated and long-range increases underestimated by these figures. Based on crime statistics in the *Statistisches Jahrbüch* and in the official *Regierungs-Blatt* for 1831 to 1841.

16. The major exception to this occurred during the first few years of the series; the *Compte général*, 1880, p. xxii ff. leaves out the period before 1836 in its summary because of legislative changes. In 1826-30, for instance, thefts of harvests were classified with thefts rather than with rural offences. Some changes in the criminal system in general are discussed by Paul Caullet, *Cours de police administrative et judiciaire* (Paris, 1928), p. 473.

17. On a semi-logarithmic graph, both absolute numbers and percentage change are directly indicated. For example, a rise from 100 to 150 and a rise from 1,000 to 1,500, both of which are increases of 50 per cent, will both be indicated by a vertical rise of the same distance on semi-log paper. Thus equal slopes also indicate equal rates of change. Data for the years 1870-1 are left out of all French series. A fire during this period destroyed many records, causing crime statistics for these years to be underestimated. See *Compte général*, 1880, p. viii.

18. It should be noted that a straight-line trend on semi-log paper indicates an exponential, not a constant, growth rate.

19. There was a short break in the rate of increase between 1866 and 1872, but it seems temporary and may have been a distortion in the census of 1872 due to the dislocations of 1870-1. See Dupeux, *La société française*, pp. 21-2.

20. The possibility that this apparent damping of cycles was the result of judicial procedures is discussed in the next chapter. Unfortunately the possible damping of cycles cannot be checked through the use of non-court records because the only such records available for Germany are for rather small areas, and the small numbers involved in such series inevitably cause a high variability in indexes.

21. Data from 'Regierungs-Blatt für das Königreich Württemberg' (1834-48).

22. See Thomas, *Social Aspects of the Business Cycle* (London, 1925), pp. 135-44. This conclusion is generally affirmed by Tobias, *Urban Crime*, p. 244, using non-quantitative sources but interestingly the more recent statistical study by Gatrell and Hadden, 'Criminal Statistics', p. 369, did in fact find a connection.

23. Any time-series contains a secular trend as well as seasonal, cyclical and residual components. For discussions of methods and problems of time-series analysis see Wesley C. Mitchell, *Business Cycles: The Problem and its Setting* (New York, 1927), pp. 261-70; William I. Greenwald, *Statistics for Economics* (Columbus, Ohio, 1963); Robert D. Mason, *Statistical Techniques in Business and Economics* (Homewood, Ill., 1970); Robert H. Wessel and Edward R. Willett, *Statistics as Applied to Economics and Business* (New York, 1959); K.A. Yeomans, *Introducing Statistics: Statistics for the Social Scientist*, 1 (Harmondsworth, England, 1968), pp. 208-44.

24. Sources of economic and demographic data for this and other computer analyses are included in the bibliography. A description of sources and indexes is provided in Appendix A—5. Twenty-six non-crime indexes were included in this particular analysis. For this series, a minimum coefficient of ± 0.22 is required to be significant at the 0.05 level.

25. The proportion of variance in a dependent variable which can be mathematically 'explained' by the variance in an independent variable (i.e. the co-

efficient of determination) = r^2. Note, however, that a correlation – even a high correlation – and consequently the fact that a certain percentage of one variable can be mathematically 'explained' by another variable in no way proves a cause-and-effect relationship between these variables; it only says that they more-or-less vary together and thus the movement in one variable can to some extent 'predict' the movement in the other.

26. The correlation was also negative in Germany. The problem of alcohol and crime is discussed in more detail in the following chapter.

27. See Zehr, 'Patterns of Crime', p. 502.

28. These correlations must be considered only approximate, since the trend which was eliminated for each period was a segment of the single linear trend for the entire century.

29. Although the upward hump in theft rates between about 1887 and 1896, if moved back a year, corresponds remarkably to the shape of the curve in bread prices.

30. Some 45 non-crime indexes were included in the analysis, but only the most important results are included here. Fuller results may be found in Appendix A–7. For this series, a minimum r of +0.35 is necessary for a significance level of 0.05.

31. See multiple regression summaries in Zehr, 'Patterns of Crime', Appendix.

32. One of the most sophisticated studies is James F. Short, Jr., 'An Investigation of the Relationship Between Crime and Business Cycles'. (Unpublished Ph.D. dissertation, University of Chicago, 1951).

33. The highest correlations were with industrial imports (r= –0.20 for the entire period, –0.45 for the early period alone) in France and with employment (r= –0.60) in Germany. Neither correlation is very significant in itself; the French correlation is rather low, and the German one is based on data for a very few years. Nevertheless, these correlations are consistent with the hypothesised connection. Fuller results may be found in Appendix A–7 and in Zehr, 'Patterns of Crime', Tables 3-8 and 3-9.

34. See, for example, Shepard Bancroft Clough, *France: A History of National Economics 1789-1939* (New York, 1964), and Jean Lescure, *Les crises générales et périodiques de surproduction* 1, 5th ed. (Paris, 1938).

35. This periodisation, developed by Arthur A. Spiethoff, is summarised in Gerhard Bry, *Wages in Germany 1871-1945* (Princeton, 1960), Appendix B, pp. 474 ff.

36. The slopes of the graph were arrived at by assigning relative numbers on the vertical scale to each phase of the cycle. A boom is characterised here by a rise of 10 points in a year, while a primary rise was assigned 1, a secondary rise 6, a capital shortage 0 (thus a plateau on the graph), and a recession = –7.

37. See Bry, *Wages*, pp. 326 and 361.

38. The coefficient of variability (v = standard deviation/mean) for real wheat prices was 0.26 in the period 1831-69 as opposed to only 0.12 in 1872-1910. Similarly, for real bread prices the coefficient was 0.21 in the early period and 0.10 later.

39. Average theft rates 1895-9 were included for correlation with indexes which were only available for the 1890s. The minimum r to be significant at the 0.05 level in this analysis is +0.21. Interrelationships among indexes are discussed in Zehr, 'Patterns of Crime', Appendix A–8. Fuller results of the correlations as well as regressions are available in Appendix A–7 and A–8.

40. Young persons are usually assumed to be more likely to commit crimes than older persons, while men – at least then – were considered more likely than women and single men more likely than married men. Thus differences in

proportions of such crime-prone groups could affect theft rates, though in France the effect appears to have been negligible. The highest correlation was with the proportion of young males, but this still explains only 8 per cent of the variance in theft. And the correlation between theft and proportions of women was not only low but positive, just opposite the expected result. For a discussion of alcohol consumption, see Appendix A–9.

41. See Zehr, 'Patterns of Crime', pp. 231-3.

42. Large cities are defined here as cities of at least 10,000 persons. Other variables include measures of overall urbanism (2,000+), population density, proportions of young people, and changes in urbanism 1875-90. Problems in the German data include the lack of social-economic data for reasonably small geographic units and the lack of regional statistics of persons tried after 1890. Results are provided in Appendix A–7.

43. Hans Herman Burchardt, *Kriminalität in Stadt und Land* (Berlin, 1936), p. 142. See also *Statistik des deutschen Reichs*, Neue Folge 23, p. II.22.

44. Exceptions were in Lübeck and Bremen. *Statistik des deutschen Reichs*, Neue Folge 45, pp. II.17-18. cf. Burchardt, *Kriminalität*, pp. 139-40.

45. More descriptive data may be found in Zehr, 'Patterns of Crime', p. 489. Raw crime statistics come from the annual *Compte général*. Where appropriate, statistics of persons tried in assize and in the lower correctional courts have been combined. Rates are per 100,000 total inhabitants due to the lack of age-specific statistics for earlier years. Population statistics for census years may be found in the *Annuaire statistique*, Retrospective Edition 1961, pp. 14-17. Between census years population figures were found by interpolation.

46. Sources of Württemberg crime statistics have been cited previously. Population statistics were culled from the *Württembergische Jahrbücher für Statistik und Landeskunde*, 1892-1912. Stuttgart has been eliminated from all population figures since it had separate, federal criminal police.

47. Further data describing these and other selected German areas may be found in the Appendix and in Zehr, 'Patterns of Crime', p. 490. See also Wolfgang Köllmann, 'The Process of Urbanization in Germany at the Height of the Industrialization Period', *Journal of Contemporary History*, 4 (July 1969), pp. 59-76.

48. Crime statistics for these cities come from published administrative reports (*Verwaltungsberichte*) and/or *Statistische Jahrbücher* for these cities. In addition, archival material is available for Bochum, Düsseldorf and Duisberg. More complete references are provided in the Bibliography. Population statistics come from the same source as well as from *Statistik des deutschen Reichs*, Band 25, Table IV; Neue Folge 32, Table IV; Neue Folge 151, Table XX; from *Statistisches Jahrbüch für den Preussischen Staat*, 1906-12; from *Statistisches Handbuch für den Preussischen Staat*, Band IV, Tables II and XI; and from *Statistisches Jahrbuch deutscher Städt*, I-XX.

49. Detailed descriptions of these areas may be found in E.A. Wrigley, *Industrial Growth and Population Change: A Regional Study in North-West Europe in the Later 19th Century* (Cambridge, England, 1962), pp. 12-30 and 38-94. Raw crime statistics come from annual *Kriminalstatistik* in *Statistik des deutschen Reichs*. Population data is based upon statistics in *ibid.*, Neue Folge 155, pp. III.139-45; Neue Folge 185, pp. II.66-7; Neue Folge 257, pp. II.76-7.

50. André Lauriot, *La police à Paris et en province* (Paris, 1904), pp. 64-8, discusses the special status of Marseilles and Lyon.

51. See Zehr, 'Patterns of Crime', p. 489.

52. *Ibid.*, p. 490.

53. No long-term crime series was available for Breslau.
54. Though the apparent upturn was much less marked for Düsseldorf than for the other three.
55. Statistics based on Wrigley, *Industrial Growth*, pp. 42, 69-70.
56. Numerous examples of this attitude could be cited. An interesting and recent case in point, however, is Louis Chevalier, *Classes laborieuses et classes dangereuses à Paris pendant la première moitié du XIXe siècle* (Paris, 1958).

Chapter 3

1. Brief surveys of the anti-urban bias among nineteenth- and twentieth-century writers are provided by George Rudé, *Debate on Europe 1815-1850* (New York, 1972), pp. 72-80, and by Carl E. Schorske, 'The Idea of the City in European Thought: Voltaire to Spengler', in Oscar Handlin and John Burchard (eds.), *The Historian and the City*, (Cambridge, Mass., 1967), pp. 95-114.
2. For criminal violence examples of such evidence may be found in Andrew F. Henry and James F. Short, Jr., *Suicide and Homicide: Some Economic and Sociological Aspects of Aggression* (New York, 1968), pp. 90-1. See also George B. Vold, 'Crime in City and Country Areas', *Annals of the American Academy of Political and Social Science*, 217 (September 1941), pp. 38-45, and Karl O. Christiansen, 'Industrialization and Urbanization in Relation to Crime and Juvenile Delinquency', *International Review of Criminal Policy*, 16 (October 1960), pp. 7-8. Recent work on collective violence is usefully summarised by Rudé, *The Debate on Europe*, pp. 80-7.
3. In addition to the sources dealing with this issue which have been previously cited, Henry and Short, *Suicide and Homicide*, pp. 134-40, provides a useful summary of findings for violence.
4. Mayr, *Geschichte der Gerichtlichen Polizei*, p. 41.
5. Bonger, *Criminality*, pp. 625-8.
6. In many German cities, and even in such large areas as a French department, the annual number of homicides averaged less than ten, and often no homicides were recorded at all. Even in Paris the annual number of homicides rarely topped one hundred during the late nineteenth century. Clearly, therefore, numbers were too low on a local or regional level to allow significant conclusions.
7. The general categories of *coups et blessures* and *Körperverletzung* appear to be roughly comparable and to include both assault and battery. Exact titles vary somewhat, however, in the various records. The term assault in this essay refers to the general category of assault and battery. Sources for indexes in this chapter are the same as those for the preceding chapter unless otherwise noted.
8. Statistics of collective violence for the 'forties and 'fifties may be found in Charles Tilly 'How Protest Modernized in France 1845-55', in William O. Aydelotte *et al.* (ed.), (Princeton, 1972), pp. 211, 243. Tilly's statistics for the rest of the century are shown in Zehr, 'Patterns of Crime', pp. 319 and 321.
9. It can, of course, be argued that France began a 'second' industrial revolution or even that it only began its real industrial revolution in the 1890s. Nevertheless, industrialisation did have a great initial impact prior to 1870. Moreover, urban population growth rates were higher in the early period than later. See Dupeux, *La société française*, pp. 21-2, and David Landes, 'Technological Change', pp. 463-4.
10. Only 20 per cent of the population of Bavaria east of the Rhine lived in cities

of 2,000 or more inhabitants (or 500 or more families) in 1861. In 1852, nearly 70 per cent of the population was engaged in agriculture or forestry, and the proportion did not dip below 50 until the first decade of the present century. *Beiträge zur Statistik* XIII: 21; Hugo Franz Brachelli, *Deutsche Staatenkunde*, I (Vienna, 1856), pp. 461-2; Julius Luebeck, *Die wirtschaftliche Entwicklung Bayerns und die Verwaltung von Handel, Industrie und Gewerbe* (Munich, 1919), pp. 19-21.

11. See, for instance, J.R. Clapham, *Economic Development of France and Germany 1815-1914* (Cambridge, England, 1961), pp. 278, 285, and Koppel S. Pinson, *Modern Germany*, pp. 221-5.

12. See, for example, H.A. Phelps, 'Cycles of Crime', *Journal of Criminal Law and Criminology*, 20 (May-June 1929), p. 115.

13. The coefficient of correlation between the two detrended indexes was r= −0.43 before 1870 as opposed to r= −0.09 after.

14. Sources of the indexes in this chapter are the same as in Chapter 2.

15. This explanation is considered by most older works on crime. See, for instance, Bonger, *Criminality*, pp. 357-73, and Gustav Aschaffenburg, *Crime and its Repression*, translated by Adalbert Albrecht (Boston, 1913), Chapter 6. That contemporary opinion saw a connection between these phenomena is illustrated by a bi-monthly report from the Prefect of Creuse to the Ministry of the Interior dated 11 January 1855 (Archives Nationales MSS, F^{IC} III Creuse 8) in which it is noted that an all-time low in crime coincided with a high in wine prices and a drop in alcohol consumption in cabarets.

16. Michael R. Marrus, 'Social Drinking in the *Belle Epoque*', *Journal of Social History*, 7 (Winter 1974), pp. 115-41.

17. Partial correlations are provided in Zehr, 'Patterns of Crime', Appendix.

18. See *ibid*.

19. Tilly's figures are provided and discussed in *ibid*., pp. 318-21. See also note 8 above. The relationship between criminal and collective violence is a topic which deserves more attention. Interpersonal violence may, for example, serve as a substitute for collective violence in situations where collective protest is not a viable option. Or, while reflecting the same underlying tensions, criminal and collective violence may tend to be participated in by different social or cultural groups. Either way, a significant connection may obtain, though the possibility is not easy to test.

20. Württemberg statistics do not include assault and battery, while statistics for this period in Baden have not been located.

21. The Bavarian situation is summarised by Theodore S. Hamerow, *Restoration, Revolution, Reaction: Economics and Politics in Germany, 1815-1871* (Princeton, 1966). See especially pp. 27-31, 146-7, 160.

22. See Richard Tilley, 'Popular Disorders in Nineteenth Century Germany: A Preliminary Survey', *Journal of Social History*, 4 (Fall 1970) pp. 1-40, and Charles, Louise and Richard Tilly, *The Rebellious Century: 1830-1930* (Cambridge, 1975). Figures are provided in Zehr, 'Patterns of Crime', p. 325.

23. The detrending method used in the computer analysis was not ideal since some indexes used in this section had distinctly curveilinear trends. Thus primary reliance is upon graphical rather than correlative analysis. Local indexes may be found in Figs. 2.19 to 2.22 and Figs. 3.10 to 3.13.

24. Correlations between rates of assault and wheat, rye, and potato prices for the period as a whole were r= −0.41, −0.30, and −0.24 respectively.

25. Correlation coefficients were high, but this was due to the presence of highly non-linear trends.

26. See, for example, the estimates of costs of living for four Ruhr cities in

Gerhard Bry, *Wages in Germany*, pp. 354-5. Price indexes for some cities (e.g. Düsseldorf) are available in yearly yearbooks or administrative reports.

27. The mean rate in Germany was 247.86 and the standard deviation was 119.90. In France in 1900-9, the mean assault rate among 86 departments was 104.20, with a standard deviation of 57.08.

28. Sources are provided in Chapter 2, notes 43-4.

29. A more detailed breakdown of departmental averages is provided in Zehr, 'Patterns of Crime', Appendix. Complete results of the correlational analysis can also be found there.

30. Using stepwise multiple regression, these are the first variables selected. See *ibid.*

31. Departmental growth rates are summarised in *ibid.*, Appendix.

32. Rates rose again during the last few years of the period but whether this was the beginning of a new trend is impossible to extrapolate.

33. The rate of reported homicides in France was 3.08. Only criminal homicides (including parricide and poisoning) are included here; negligent or involuntary manslaughter is excluded.

34. While commercially produced hand-guns were perhaps not widely and readily available even then, the wonderful array of such weapons – both homemade and factory-produced – taken from offenders and preserved in the police museum in Paris attests to their availability and use.

35. Taken together, initial levels of homicide and levels of alcohol consumption explain 76 per cent of the variance in homicide 1900-4.

36. The relationship between suicide and homicide is of some importance; some students have suggested, for instance, that both types of violence are rooted in the same causes but reflect different cultural or class response to these pressures. For a full discussion see Zehr, 'Patterns of Crime', pp. 367-75. See also Sheldon Hackney, 'Southern Violence', in *Violence in America*, pp. 479-500, and Henry and Short, *Suicide and Homicide*.

37. The suicide-homicide ratio (SHR=100 x Hom./Hom. + Suic). Suicide statistics are derived from Ministry of Justice figures in the *Compte général*. The SHR was calculated using persons tried rather than cases reported for homicide in order to avoid the cases *v.* persons problem. The highest correlation during the early period was with the general price index (r= −0.85) though the correlation with wine consumption was also high (r= 0.71). Similar comparisons are impossible for Germany due to the lack of good suicide statistics until the very end of the period.

38. Again, however, the small numbers of homicides involved – and thus the importance of a random element in this index – must be emphasised.

39. Other results may be found in the Appendix.

40. As is discussed later, the relationship between the TVR and urbanism was not linear. Thus the coefficient would be higher if non-linear correlational methods were used.

41. The TVR is based on convictions for theft and/or serious assault only. Sources have been provided previously. Major *Stadtkreise* were urban districts containing cities of 20,000 or more persons.

42. Also, average TVRs in static rural departments were quite similar to, though slightly higher than, average ratios in modernising areas, but both were higher than ratios in older, more static urban departments. See Zehr, 'Patterns of Crime', Appendix.

43. Offences against agents of the state (*rebellion* in France, *Widerstand* in Germany), however, were higher in cities than in the countryside, but, like other forms of criminal violence, do appear to have risen during the initial stages of modernisation. See Appendix. A–7 and *ibid.*, pp. 395-415.

44. The general conclusions in point 5-7 are remarkably similar to those of Henry and Short, *Suicide and Homicide*. In their study of American data, violence was positively related to the business cycle (see pp. 15, 45, 55), but they also concluded that alcohol consumption was not sufficient to explain the correlation (see pp. 15, 45, 47, 51, 64).
45. *Ibid.*, pp. 90-1.
46. *Ibid.*
47. It should be noted, however, that the actual relationship may be somewhat more complex than this suggests; suicide, for instance, was found by Henry and Short to react differently to different parts of the business cycle.
48. Henry and Short, *Suicide and Homicide*, pp. 92-4.

Chapter 4

1. *Annuaire Statistique de la France*, Retrospective Edition, 1961, p. 78.
2. Based on data in the *Uniform Crime Reports for the United States* for 1951 and 1952 (No. 1, pp. 4-5), 1967 (pp. 96-7), and 1973 (p. 59). Ratios based on murder, aggravated assault, burglary, larceny; they exclude auto theft, simple assault and robbery.
3. J.J. Tobias, *Urban Crime*, pp. 122, 244. It should be noted that, on the surface, Charles, Richard and Louise Tilly's conclusions in *The Rebellious Century*, pp. 79-80, would seem to support Tobias nicely. That these results are seriously in error is pointed out in Chapter 1, Note 11.
4. *Ibid.*, pp. 122-47, 244.
5. *Ibid.*, pp. 244-55.
6. E.J. Hobsbawn, Primitive Rebels: *Studies in Archaic Forms of Social Movement in the 19th and 20th Centuries* (New York, 1965).
7. For discussions of the political nature of crime, see E.O. Wright, *The Politics of Punishment*.

APPENDIX

This investigation has relied upon statistical analysis of some rather novel sources, and raises a number of questions about methodology and sources. A few of these have been dealt with in the text, and the following appendix contains a bit more information about sources (A–5) and methods (A–1 to A–3) as well as fuller results of computations. However, due to limitations of space the material in the appendix and bibliography remains illustrative rather than exhaustive; more complete data may be found in my Ph.D. dissertation, on file at Rutgers University Library and with Xerox University Microfilms, Ann Arbor, Michigan.

A 1. The Constructions of Crime Rates

The construction of usable crime indexes poses a number of problems, some of which have been mentioned in the text. Most obvious, of course, are questions of what distortions crime statistics contain and what sorts of categories to use. A further methodological problem, however, has to do with the calculation of rates. Obviously, simple comparisons of raw crime statistics would be meaningless; to adjust for variations in population, raw crime statistics must be converted into rates per unit of the population. But what population? Police or even court records often do no specify the exact area and population included in their jurisdiction. Census data are not always divisible into the desired areas and, at any rate, are only available for census years. Nor are census data entirely accurate, especially since transients and non-resident workers, whose criminal potential may differ from that of the resident population, are not consistently included, and this can be an important omission in areas such as western Germany where railroads allowed workers to reside some distance from their places of work. And this suggests a further problem. Most crime rates are determined per unit of the total resident population. But certain population groups are more likely to commit crimes than others. Although this is now changing, women traditionally have been less likely to commit most crimes than men, and married men somewhat less likely than unmarried. Very young children presumably do not commit many crimes and, when they do, their offences are not likely to appear in crime records. Certain age cohorts, such as the 15-30 age-group, have higher rates of

offences than others. Some crimes appear to be more characteristic of
one social class than another. Crime rates, then, might appear to be
higher in one area than another or to rise through time simply because
of a higher percentage of high-risk groups in the population.

Ideally, therefore, rates should be constructed in such a way as to
correct not only for differences in total population size but also for
differences in age, family, sex and class structures. Unfortunately, however a single index which would adjust for these demographic factors
is impractical, both because of the difficulty of incorporating all of
these variables into a simple index and because such data are frequently
lacking, at least in usable form, for many areas in the nineteenth century. The rates used here, therefore, are necessarily crude. Where
possible, rates have at least been calculated per 100,000 adults. This is
particularly important for indexes based on court records since by law
or custom children under 10 or 12 usually did not usually appear in
court in either Germany or France. Useful age data are frequently
unavailable, however, and rates per 100,000 of the total population
often have been unavoidable. Correlation and regression analysis must
be relied upon to provide some estimate of the effect of age and sex
variables upon rates. Population figures for non-census years have been
estimated by either arithmetic or geometric interpolation, depending
upon number of years between censuses.

A-2.

Percentage of Crimes Known to Public Prosecutors Which Did
Not Go to Trial in France During the Nineteenth Century

	1846- 50	1861- 65	1876- 80	1886- 90	1891- 95	1896- 1900
Homicide	60.1%	58.2%	59.7%	61.7%	61.1%	62.5%
Assault & Battery	54.3	43.5	47.0	48.8	48.2	47.8
Theft	53.5	57.1	64.3	68.5	71.3	73.7
Fraud-Embezzlement	56.8	54.4	65.9	71.7	76.0	78.2

Based on *Compte général*, Table 21, volumes 1880 and 1900. The most important reasons for dropping cases in 1876-80 were as follows:

Homicide: No indictable offence involved (40.3%), insufficient charges
                      (24.2%) and offender unknown (23.5%).
Assault: Lack of severity (51.6%).
Theft: Offender unknown (62.2%).
Fraud-Embezzlement: No indictable offence (53.3%).

A-3

Pearson Correlations Between Fluctuations in Persons Tried and Cases
Reported in France, 1831-1910. Linear Trend Removed

	1831-1900 r=	1831-69 r=	1872-1910 r=
Homicide	.92	.94	.87
Assault and Battery	.84	.92	.70
Theft	.82	.91	.69

City and Departmental Profiles

A4a. EIGHT FRENCH DEPARTMENTS

	Creuse	Vendée	Loir-et-Cher	Loire	Pas-de-Calais	Nord	Bouches-du-Rhône	Seine
Urban Percentage 1906	11.0	16.4	19.9	53.6	49.7	70.7	86.6	99.6
Change in urban percentage, 1876-1906	1.0	2.9	− 0.6	7.4	15.1	12.4	5.2	1.1
Change in urban proportions 1876-1906 as percentages of 1876 level	+ 9.0	+27.0	− 3.0	+ 16.0	+44.0	+21.0	+ 6.0	+ 1.0
Percentage growth in total urban pop. 1876-1906	+8.0	+31.0	− 2.0	+27.0	+83.0	+51.0	+46.0	+62.0
Percentage of pop. in cities 10,000 + in 1906	0	8.0	9.0	38.0	28.0	44.0	79.0	96.0
Pop. change 1876-1906 as percentages	− 2.0	+ 8.0	+ 1.0	+ 9.0	+ 28.0	+ 25.0	+ 38.0	+ 60.0
Pop. density, 1906 (pop. per sq. km)	48.9	63.1	43.0	134.2	150.0	328.4	145.9	8026.3
Change in density, 1876-1906	− 2.0	+ 3.0	0	+ 8.0	+ 25.0	+ 23.0	+ 34.0	+ 59.0
Percentage of active pop. in industry 1901	19.5	20.6	24.1	57.3	49.6	64.2	54.9	55.2
Percentage increase in pop.:								
1831-51	8.3	16.4	11.0	21.0	5.8	17.0	19.5	52.1
1851-72	− 4.2	4.4	2.7	16.5	9.8	25.0	29.4	56.1
1872-91	3.6	10.2	4.1	11.8	14.8	19.9	13.7	41.5
1891-1911	6.7	− 0.7	− 3.2	4.1	22.2	13.0	27.7	32.2

A4b FOURTEEN GERMAN CITIES OR DISTRICTS

	Approximate population in 1910, in 1,000s[a]		Population growth 1885-1910[b]
			%
New Industrial Cities			
Dusseldorf	353		212
Bochum	137		234
Duisborg	229		377
Oberhausen	90		350
Large old cities			
Berlin	2059		59
Breslau	512		71
Smaller cities			
Ohligs	27		108
Bonn	89		147
Mülheim-am-Rhein	53		112
Württemberg districts			
Neckarkreis[c]	70%	(53%)	38
Schwarzwaldkreis	43%	(32%)	20
Donaukreis	43%	(31%)	20
Jagstkreis	29%	(23%)	2

[a]For the four districts of Württemberg, data are urban percentages.
Data in parentheses are urban percentages in 1885.

[b]Major territorial changes eliminated where possible, although such changes were
impossible to eliminate completely for the four industrial cities.

[c]Without Stuttgart.

A–5

Guide to Variables in Computer Programs

Basic modes of computer analysis have been indicated in the text. The following table describes the major correlative indexes or variables used in these pro-grammes. Variable identification numbers serve to identify these variables in Tables A–1 and A–8. Source numbers refer to the list of statistical sources provided at the end of this table (A–5e). In the case of a composite index, the source listing includes only sources not previously given in connection with another index from which it is composed.

A–5a FRANCE: TIME-SERIES ANALYSIS

Based on annual national figures 1827–1910 (without 1870-1) with linear trend removed for correlational purposes.

Variable Identification Number	Variable Name/Description	Source of Raw Data
		Compte général
1–5	Crime indexes (persons tried, reports) and ratio calculated per 100,000 persons 10 years and older	F6
6	Wholesale industrial price index	F2
7	Wholesale food price index	F2
8	General wholesale price index ((no. 6+ no. 7)/2)	
9	Estimated hourly wages	F10
10	Beef prices, wholesale, per kg	F9
11	Real beef prices (10/9)	
12	Wholesale wheat prices per quintal	F9
13	Real wheat prices (12/9)	
14	Bread prices per kg in Paris	F9
15	Real bread prices (14/9)	
16	Wholesale rye price per quintal	F9
17	Real rye prices (16/9)	
18	Potato prices per quintal	F1 (1913)
19	Real potato prices (18/9)	
20	Potato consumption *per capita* (quintal)	F1 (1913)
21	Wine consumption (litres *per capita*)	F1 (1913)
22	Coal production, 1,000s of tons	F2
23	Cast iron production, 1,000s of tons	F2
24	Import of finished goods, value in francs	F2
25	Import of raw goods, value in francs	F2
26	Total industrial imports (24+25)	
27	Annual mean temperature, centigrade	F2
28	Real wage index	F8
29	Average yearly wages of miners (combustible materials)	F1 (1913)
30	Annual strikes (1890 ff. only)	F1 (1913)
31	Strikers per year, in thousands	F1 (1913)

A-5b FRANCE: CROSS-SECTIONAL ANALYSIS

Based on data for 86 departments at the beginning of the twentieth century.

Variable Identification Number	Variable Name/Description	Source of Raw Data
		Compte Générale,
1—4	Crime indexes and ratios; emphasis upon 1900-4 but also including 1838-40, 1895-9, 1900-2	F2, F4
5	Trends in crime (rates in 1900-2 — rates in 1838-40)/rates in 1838-40)	
6	Population density per sq. km, 1906	F1 (1907)
7	Percentage change in pop. density, 1876-1906 ((density 1906 — density 1876)/density 1876)	F1 (1907, (1879)
8	Rates of young people (10-30 yrs.) per 10,000, 1901	F4
9	Women per 10,000 men, 1901	F4
10	Percentage of men 18-95 years who were married in 1901	F4
11	Percentage of the population that was foreign-born, 1906	F4
12	Percentage change in proportion foreign-born, 1876-1906 ((foreign 1906 — foreign 1876)/foreign 1876)	F4
13	Urban percentage (2,000+) 1906	F4
14	Urban percentage, 1901	F4
15	Difference in urban percentage 1876 to 1906 (% urban 1906 — % urban 1876)	F4, F1 (1879)
16	Percentage change in urban proportions 1876-1906 (15/% urban 1876)	
17	Difference in urban percentage 1901-6 (% urban 1906 — %urban 1901)	
18	Percentage change in urban proportion 1901-6 (17/% urban 1901)	
19	Percentage growth in total urban population 1876-1906 ((total urban pop. 1906 — total urban pop. 1876)/ total urban pop. 1876)	F4, F1 (1879)
20	Percentage of total population living in cities larger than 10,000 persons, 1906	F4
21	Percentage of active population engaged in industry, 1901	F4
22	Difference in percentage of industrial population 1896-1901 (% ind. 1901 — % ind. 1896)	F4
23	Percentage change in percentage of indust. pop. 1896-1901 (22/% indust. 1896)	
24	Factory workers as percentage of active wage earners in establishments with 100+ wage-earners, 1901(A)	F4
25	Factory workers as percentage of total active persons in establishments of more than 100 wage-earners, 1901(B)	F4
26	Difference in percentage of factory workers 1896-1901 (no. 24 — factory workers 1896)	F4
27	Percentage difference in proportion of factory workers (no. 26/% factory workers 1896)	
28	Unemployed per 10,000 wage-earners, 1901	F4

Variable Identification Number	Variable Name/Description	Source of Raw Data
29	Average day wages for male workers, 1891-3	F1, (1898)
30	Prices per kg of white bread, 1903	F1, (1904)
31	Prices per kg of brown bread, 1903	F1, (1904)
32	Prices per kg of mixed bread, 1903	F1, (1904)
33	Prices per kg of white bread, 1896	F1, (1898)
34	Prices per kg of beef, 1896	F1, (1898)
35	Wine consumption *per capita*, 1901	F1, (1902)
36	Total alcohol consumption *per capita*, 1901 (wine+cider+'alcohols')	F1, (1902)
37	Percentage population change 1876-1906 ((Pop. 1906 $\triangle$ pop. 1876)/pop. 1876)	
38	Absolute percentage population change 1876-1906, i.e. ignoring direction of change	
39	Illiteracy as percentage of recruits who could neither read nor write	F1, (1902)
40	Percentage of recruits who could barely read and write	F1, (1902)

A5c. GERMANY: TIME-SERIES ANALYSIS

Based on national figures 1882-1912, with linear trend removed for correlative purposes.

Variable Identification Number	Variable Name/Description	Source of Raw Data
1—5	Crime rates (persons tried) and ratios calculated per 100,000 punishable persons	G2, G1
6	Average earnings in industry, transport and distribution	G4
7	Cost of living index	G4
8	Food cost index	G4
9	Pork price index	G4
10	Wheat bread price index	G4
11	Rye bread price index	G4
12	Wheat flour price index	G4
13	Potato price index	G4
14	Share price index	G4
15	Volume of imported finished goods, index	G5
16	Volume of total imported goods	G5
17	Volume of imported raw materials	G5
18	Volume of half-finished imports	G5
19	Index of total industrial production	G5
20	Index of iron and steel castings production	G5
21	Index of coal production, hard and soft	G5
22	Beer consumption	G5
23	Potato consumption	G5

Variable Identification Number	Variable Name/Description	Source of Raw Data
24	Average yearly income, all sectors, in marks	G5
25	Yearly industrial income	G5
26	Yearly miners' wages	G5
27	Yearly agricultural workers' income	G5
28	Yearly domestic servants' income	G5
29	Real investment in building	G5
30	Producers' price of wheat/ton	G5
31	Wholesale pork prices	G5
32	Producers' prices for agricultural products	G5
33	Index of industrial production (population constant, some years missing)	G6
34	Index of agricultural production (population constant, some years missing)	G6
35	Wholesale price index	G3
36	Real national income (incomplete series)	G3
37	Employment rates, unions, as percentage (incomplete series)	G3
38	Average weekly industrial wage index	G3
39	Index of average weekly real industrial wages	G3
40	Annual number of strikes and lockouts (1899-1912)	G2
41	Annual number of strikers (1892-1912)	G2
42	Man-days lost in strikes and lockouts	G3
43	Transoceanic migration per 1,000 inhabitants	G1
44	Real earnings (nos. 6/7)	
45	Average strike size (nos. 41/40)	
46	Real pork price index (nos. 9/38)	
47	Real wheat bread price index (nos. 10/38)	
48	Real rye bread price (nos. 11/38)	
49	Real potato price index (nos. 13/38)	
50	Real food prices: A: nos. 8/38 B: nos. 8/6 C: nos. 8/24	

A5d. GERMANY: CROSS-SECTIONAL ANALYSIS

Based on data for 83 *Regierungs-Bezirke* around 1890

Variable Identification Number	Variable Name/Description	Source of Raw Data
1–2	Crime rates (persons tried) and TVR calculated per 100,000 punishable persons, 1885-1890	G2
3	Persons 15-40 years of age per 1,000 persons	G2
4	Population density per sq. km	G2
5	Percentage of population living in large cities (20,000+)	G2
6	Percentage of population living in cities (2,000+)	G2
7	Change in proportion of population living in cities, 1875-90	G2
8	Percentage change in proportion urban ((% urban 1890 − % urban 1875)/ % urban 1875)	

A5e. MAJOR SOURCES OF CORRELATIVE DATA CITED IN PRECEDING
TABLE

Source   Source
Identification
Number

France

F1   *Annuaire Statistique de la France,* (1878-1913) (Paris)
F2   *Annuaire Statistique de la France,* Retrospective edition, 1961
            (Paris).
F3   *Compte générale de l'administration de la justice criminelle en
            France,* (1827-1910) (Paris).
F4   *Résultats statistiques du recensement général de la population,*
            (1881, 1891, 1901, 1911) (Paris).
F5   *Statistique de la France,* deuxième série: I-XXI; nouvelle série:
            1811-1913 (Paris).
            [Industrial census: deuxième série XIX;
            Population censuses: deuxième série I-II, XIII, XXI.]
F6   Bourgeois-Pichat, J., 'The General Development of the Population
            of France since the 18th Century', in David Glass and D.E.
            Eversley (eds.), *Population in History: Essays in Historical
            Demography,* (Chicago, 1965).
F7   Crouzet, François, 'An Annual Index of French Industrial Produc-
            tion in the 19th Century', pp. 245-78, in Rondo Cameron,
            Essays in French Economic History, (Georgetown, Ontario,
            1970).
F8   Dupreiz Leon H, *Des mouvements économiques généraux,* 2 vols.
            (Louvain, 1947).
            'Evolution de la population active en France depuis cent ans d'après
            de dénombrements quinquenaux', *Etudes et Conjonctures*
            (May-June 1953), pp. 230-88.
F9   Fourastié, Jean, *Documents pour l'histoire et la théorie des prix,*
            2 vols. (Paris).
F10   ——, *L'évolution des prix à long terme,* (Paris, 1969).

Germany

G1   *Statistische Jahrbuch für das deutsche Reich,* Vols. I-XXXIV,
            (Berlin, 1880-1913).
G2   *Statistik des deutschen Reichs,* Erste Reihe I-LXIII (1873-83),
            Neue Folge 1-149 (1884-1903), without prefix 150- (1903-)
            (Berlin).
            [Population census: ER II, XIV, LVII; NF 68, 150, 151, 240.
            Industrial and occupational censuses: ER XXXIV and XXXV;
            NF 2-7, 102-19, 202-22.]
G3   Bry, Gerhard, *Wages in Germany 1871-1945,* (Princeton, 1960).
G4   Desai, Ashok, *Real Wages in Germany 1871-1913,* (Oxford, 1968).
G5   Hoffman Walter G., *Das Wachstum der deutschen Wirtschaft Seit
            der Mitte des 19 Jahrhunderts,* (Berlin, 1965).
G6   Dessirier, Jean, 'Indices comparés de la production industrielle et de
            production agricole en divers pays de 1870 à 1928', *Bulletin de
            la statistique générale de la France et du service d'observations
            des prix*, 18 (October-December 1928), pp. 65-112.

A-6.

Significance Levels

Minimum r required to be significant at various standard significance levels for the four major computer programmes. Values approximate.

French time-series analysis 1827-1910
(based on 78 years)

	German cross-sectional analysis (83 *Regierungs-Bezirke*)		
Significance level	.05	.01	.001
Minimum r(+)	.22	.28	.36

	French cross-sectional analysis 86 departments		
Significance level	.05	.01	.001
Minimum r(+)	.21	.27	.34

	Germany time-series analysis 1882-1912 (based on 31 years)		
Significance level	.05	.01	.001
	.35	.45	.55

A−7.

Pearson Correlations

A7a. FRANCE: Cross-sectional correlations (r) between average crime rates 1900-4 (persons tried) and miscellaneous demographic and economic variables, 86 departments. (A guide to variable identification numbers may be found in A −5b, while levels of significance are provided in A−6.)

Variable I.D No.	Theft	Homicide	Assault	TVR	Rebellion	SHR[a]
6	.15	.02	−.08	−.28	.36	.04
9	.11	−.13	−.13	−.18	−.01	.05
10	−.20	−.29	−.35	−.10	−.27	.30
11	.41	.34	.29	−.14	.35	−.20
13	.66	.20	.16	−.56	.63	−.01
24	.38	−.10	.35	−.02	.42	.17
25	.46	−.05	.41	−.06	.47	.14
28	.26	.05	−.08	−.26	.22	−.03
35	−.03	.18	−.16	−.16	.18	−.09
29	.41	−.05	.08	−.36	.49	.23
30	.20	.25	.10	−.17	.16	−.18
32	.30	.25	.17	−.21	.30	−.14
31	.33	.40	.26	−.18	.35	−.15
33	.18	.36	.12	−.15	.19	−.30
34	.19	-.14	−.03	−.20	.12	.24
2[b]	.21	.81	.45	.41	.33	−−
14	.65	.20	.14	−.57	.63	−.01
15	.55	.09	.44	−.19	.49	.05
16	.12	−.004	.38	.20	.17	.03
17	.29	.10	.31	.01	.22	−.03
18	.05	.04	.19	.18	.05	−.05
19	.44	.16	.42	−.08	.48	−.05
20	.59	.20	.07	−.59	.53	−.04
37	.49	.22	.23	−.29	.51	−.10
38	.40	.18	.11	−.34	.39	−.09
7	.46	.23	.22	−.27	.50	−.10
22	.08	.41	.21	−.02	.06	−.40
23	−.05	.56	.24	.18	−.06	−.58
26	.06	−.05	−.09	−.16	−.01	.03
27	.04	.002	−.11	−.17	−.01	.004
12	.03	.11	.10	.03	.13	−.12
36	.70	.29	.41	−.38	.60	.15
39	−.09	.04	−.01	.19	−.19	−.08
40	−.05	.13	.05	.09	−.05	−.16
8 (total)	.23	.21	.32	.11	.28	−.21
21	.68	.09	.42	−.32	.71	.14
8 (male)	.28	.18	.36	.06	.36	−.15

[a]Note that this SHR is calculated just opposite from the formula shown in the text; here, SHR = 100 x Suicide/(Suicide + Homicide)
[b]Same crime, 1838-40

(1870-1 excluded, linear trend removed). (A guide to variable identification numbers may be found in A–5a, while levels of significance are provided in A–6.) A=1831-1910. B=1831-69 only. C=1872-1910 only. See text for limitations inherent in these figures.

Variable (ID No.)	Homicide			Assault			TVR			Theft			SHR		
	A	B	C	A	B	C	A	B	C	A	B	C	A	B	C
27	-.04	—	—	.18	.18	.24	—	—	—	-.15	-.25	-.06	—	—	—
6	-.44	-.84	.42	-.51	-.85	.05	-.42	-.72	.10	.16	.33	-.09	-.10	-.78	.70
7	-.38	-.70	.02	-.58	-.75	-.38	-.57	-.75	-.35	.32	.48	.13	-.22	-.77	.20
8	-.47	-.85	.26	-.60	-.88	-.17	-.54	-.79	-.13	.26	.42	.02	-.17	-.85	.52
10[a]	.39	.68	.03	.06	.70	-.29	-.07	.29	-.23	.20	.41	.03	.39	.60	.16
11[a]	.36	64	-.10	.04	.65	-.39	-.12	.27	-.32	.25	.38	.07	.32	.62	-.002
12	-.31	-.44	.05	-.61	-.68	-.45	-.74	-.85	-.44	.59	.76	.20	-.22	-.52	.18
13	-.34	-.45	-.01	-.60	-.65	-.50	-.74	-.83	-.49	.61	.75	.22	-.25	-.49	.11
14	-.28	-.41	-.04	-.59	-.61	-.58	-.71	-.73	-.66	.54	.60	.40	-.26	-.56	.01
15	-.36	-.47	-.16	-.60	-.61	-.65	-.72	-.73	-.71	.54	.60	.40	-.32	-.55	-.13
16[a]	.36	—	.36	-.17	—	-.17	-.22	—	-.22	.16	—	.16	.35	—	.35
17[a]	.36	—	.36	-.16	—	-.16	-.21	—	-.21	.17	—	.17	.36	—	.36
18[a]	.28	—	.28	.05	—	.05	.11	—	.11	-.11	—	-.11	.33	—	.33
19[a]	.24	—	.24	.04	—	.04	.09	—	.09	-.10	—	-.10	.26	—	.26
20	.09	.06	.12	.24	.31	.15	.17	.36	-.10	-.05	-.31	.29	.01	—	-.02
21	.44	.51	.42	.65	.86	.42	.78	.91	.67	-.60	-.66	-.56	.62	.56	.71
22	.55	.68	.36	.46	.48	.45	.40	.43	.41	-.16	-.19	-.15	.47	.41	.42
23	.46	.36	.71	.34	.14	.54	.31	.17	.49	-.19	-.11	-.19	.56	-.04	.77
24	.71	.78	.70	.44	.63	.29	.36	.53	.25	-.12	-.21	-.07	.67	.59	.68
25	.04	-.48	.50	-.05	-.28	.11	.08	.03	.14	-.20	-.38	-.10	.27	-.69	.71
26	.26	-.11	.59	.10	.01	.16	.18	.26	.18	-.20	-.45	-.10	.43	.46	.75
30[a]	.37	—	.37	.44	—	.44	-.06	—	-.06	.45	—	.45	.22	—	.22
31[a]	.05	—	.05	.26	—	.26	.13	—	.13	.13	—	.13	.10	—	.10
28	.18	.52	.23	.50	.79	.49	.61	.84	.57	-.45	-.60	-.32	.24	.57	.26
29	-.04	-.46	-.14	-.30	-.55	-.42	-.27	-.54	-.40	.13	.36	.17	.05	-.52	.06

[a] Data not available for entire period.

A.7c. GERMANY: Time-series correlations (r) between annual crime rates
(persons tried) and miscellaneous economic variables, 1882-1912 (linear trend
removed). See text for limitations inherent in these figures. (A guide to variable
identification numbers may be found in A—5c while levels of significance are
provided in A—6.)

Variable (ID No)	Homicide	Assault	Theft	TVR
6	.33	−.80	.27	−.77
7	.45	−.93	.46	−.94
8	.51	−.90	.57	−.97
9	.34	−.53	.47	−.62
10	.08	−.83	.10	−.71
11	.25	−.58	.61	−.71
12	.36	−.80	.52	−.86
13	.35	−.55	.16	−.52
14	−.24	.26	−.38	.35
15	.19	.08	.12	−.001
16	.44	−.63	.26	−.63
17	.25	−.62	.10	−.55
18	.36	−.72	.12	−.65
19	.42	−.82	.17	−.75
20	.33	−.79	.10	−.69
21	.37	−.86	.29	−.82
22	−.49	.83	−.36	.82
23	−.29	.68	−.28	.68
24	.38	−.93	.30	−.88
25	.24	−.93	.16	−.82
26	.09	−.36	.38	−.44
27	.44	−.83	.32	−.82
28	.56	−.86	.44	−.89
29	−.24	−.21	.15	−.20
30	.10	−.65	.33	−.66
31	.37	−.54	.28	−.56
32	.45	−.80	.46	−.84
35	.10	−.68	.29	−.67
38	.22	−.88	.19	−.79
39	−.69	.54	−.71	.74
43	.40	−.80	.61	−.89
33[a]	.09	−.05	−.25	.01
34[a]	−.20	.11	−.24	.04
36[a]	−.21	.10	−.24	.15
37[a]	−.12	−.006	−.60	.23
40[a]	−.22	.05	−.58	.19

Variable (ID No)	Homicide	Assault	Theft	TVR
41[a]	−.08	.01	−.59	.15
42[a]	−.10	.005	−.52	.13
45[a]	.02	.02	−.54	.13
44	−.23	.29	−.35	.37
50A	.59	−.43	.75	−.66
46	.22	.06	.40	−.11
47	−.02	−.65	.03	−.53
48	.18	−.25	.65	−.45
49	.29	−.25	.11	−.26
50B	.39	−.41	.57	−.55
50C	.50	−.46	.75	−.67

[a]Data not available for entire period.

A.7d. GERMANY: Cross-sectional correlations (r) between crime rates 1885-90 (persons tried) and several demographic variables, 83 *Regierungs-Bezirke*. (Guide to variable identification numbers provided in A--5d. Levels of significance in ∧ 6.)

	% Urban (6)	% Large urban (5)	Population density (4)	Difference in % urban 1875-90 (7)	% Change in % urban 1875-90 (8)	Proportion of young people (3)
Homicide	−.13	−.10	−.13	−.001	.10	−.09
Robbery	−.04	−.02	.03	−.12	−.08	−.04
Serious theft	.25	.38	.36	.06	−.12	.34
Minor theft	−.09	−.02	−.04	−.01	.07	−.02
Minor assault	−.15	−.05	−.11	.14	−.01	−.05
Serious assault	−.12	−.11	−.09	−.12	−.04	−.07
Total assault	−.14	−.10	−.10	−.13	−.04	−.07
Total theft	−.06	.06	.07	−.007	−.05	−.01
TVR	−.07	−.16	−.18	−.12	−.06	−.06
Opposition to authorities	.38	.39	.41	.16	−.15	.35

A–8.

Multiple Regressions

Unless otherwise noted, unaltered step-wise regression procedure has been used; independent variables have been allowed to enter in order of decreasing independent contribution to the prediction of the dependent variable. Only the variables which make significant contributions are given here; those entering later and making only slight contributions to the explanation of the dependent variable have been left out. Calculations are based on the computer programmes summarised in A–5, and variable identification numbers in parenthese refer to the variable numbers in that summary.

A8a. FRANCE: Time-series, 1831-1910, Linear Trend Removed

Independent Variable (1)	Multiple r (2)	R^2 (3)	Simple r (4)
A. Dependent Variable: *Theft*			
All variables allowed in			
Real wheat prices	.61	.37	.61
Wine consumption	.72	.53	−.60
Real beef prices	.75	.56	.25
Real wages	.80	.63	−.45
B. Dependent Variable: *Theft*			
Wine consumption kept out			
Real wheat prices	.61	.37	.61
Import − raw materials	.69	.48	−.20
Import − finished goods	.71	.50	−.12
General price index	.75	.56	.26
C. Dependent Variable: *Assault*			
All variables except rye and			
potato prices, strikes			
Wine consumption	.65	.42	.65
General price index	.84	.70	−.60
Iron production	.85	.72	.34
Real bread prices	.86	.74	−.60

A8b. FRANCE: Cross-sectional, 86 Departments, 1900-4

Independent Variable (1)	Multiple r (2)	r^2 (3)	Simple r (4)
A. Dependent Variable: *Theft* Sex and youth rates forced in first, unaltered stepwise thereafter			
Youth rate (8)	.23	.06	.23
Sex ratio (9)	.27	.07	.11
Alcohol consumption	.73	.54	.70
Urban percentage 1906	.84	.71	.66
Population density 1906	.87	.75	.15
Growth, urban population (19)	.88	.77	.44
B. Dependent Variable: *Theft* Youth and sex rates forced in first, then unaltered stepwise regression among change variables only.			
Youth rate (8)	.23	.06	.23
Sex ratio (9)	.27	.07	.11
Change in urban percentage (15)	.59	.35	.55
Absolute population change (38)	.63	.40	.40
Growth, urban populations (19)	.65	.42	.44
C. Dependent Variable: *Assault* All essential variables allowed in			
Change in urban percentage (15)	.44	.20	.44
Assault rate, 1830s (2)	.58	.34	.45
Factory workers (25)	.63	.40	.41
Change in industrial population (23)	.67	.45	.24
Alcohol consumption	.72	.51	.41
D. Dependent Variable: *Rebellion* Youth and sex rates forced in first, unaltered stepwise regression of all variables thereafter.			
Youth rate (8)	.28	.08	.28
Sex ratio (9)	.28	.08	−.01
Industrial population 1901	.72	.52	.71
Alcohol consumption	.79	.63	.60
Population growth (37)	.81	.65	.52
E. Dependent Variable: *Homicide* Economic variables kept out.			
Homicides 1830s (2)	.81	.66	.81
Alcohol consumption	.87	.76	.29
Foreign population (11)	.91	.83	.34

A8c GERMANY: Time series indexes, 1882-1910, Linear Trend Removed

Independent Variable (1)	Multiple r (2)	r^2 (3)	Simple r (4)
A. Dependent Variable: *Theft* Individual food prices kept out			
Real food prices	.75	.56	.75
Import, finished goods	.80	.65	.12
Employment rate	.88	.77	−.60
Beer consumption	.89	.79	−.36
B. Dependent Variable: *Theft* Real prices, specialised wage indexes kept out.			
Real wages	.71	.50	−.71
Rye bread prices	.79	.63	.61
Wheat bread prices	.90	.81	.10
C. Dependent Variable: *Theft* Specialised wage indexes and potato prices kept out.			
Real food prices	.75	.56	.75
Real rye bread prices	.81	.65	.65
Real wheat bread prices	.86	.74	.03

A–9.

Crime and Alcohol Consumption in France

Indexes of wine consumption and of total alcohol consumption (i.e. including wine, ciders and hard liquors) were included in the French cross sectional correlation. The results, provided below, are interesting, if somewhat confusing.

Pearson Correlations Between Crime Rates and Alcohol Consumption in France, 1900-4

	Homicide r=	Assault r=	Theft r=
Wine	.18	−.16	−.03
Total Alcohol	.29	.41	.70

That we should find a positive connection, even if relatively weak, between violence and alcohol consumption is not surprising, of course; the same relationship obtained through time and can be attributed either to the fact that drunkenness sometimes leads to violence or that both alcohol consumption and violence reflect certain underlying frustrations and/or traditions. Interestingly, though, it is total alcohol consumption rather than wine consumption which is most highly correlated cross sectionally, and this in a nation famed for its wine.*

But the most tantalising result is the high positive correlation between theft and *per capita* alcohol consumption; departments with high theft rates also tended to be those with high rates of alcohol consumption, at least as measured by official figures. A direct casual connection between these two phenomena is not totally unreasonable; alcohol could lead to theft or, as is often suggested in regard to drugs, the need for alcohol could lead men to steal. But the correlation raises some questions. Why is it higher for theft than for violence, which other studies have confirmed is often associated directly or indirectly with alcoholism? And why total alcohol rather than wine? Although a

---

* One recent study has observed signs that wine was increasingly being displaced by distilled alcohols such as aperitifs by the end of the century. See Michael R. Marrus, 'Social Drinking in the Belle Epoque', *Journal of Social History*, 7 (Winter 1974), pp. 115-41. However, this class of alcohol still made up a rather small percentage of total alcohol consumption according to official sources.

correlation obtained between wine consumption (total alcohol was not included here) and theft through time, the correlation was negative and appeared to be spurious.

Whether the cross sectional correlation between theft and alcohol consumption is real, an accident, or only spurious, the result of a secondary correlation between alcohol consumption and another better predictor of theft rates, is difficult to determine definitely. At least it can be shown that the correlation was not a spurious result of a correlation with another variable in the group. The correlation between theft and alcohol consumption was the highest in the matrix and factor analysis suggests that the variance in alcohol consumption was rather independent of other variables. Moreover, the correlation between theft and alcohol consumption, when controlled for any single variable or combination of two other variables in the group, does not drop substantially as it would if the relationship between alcohol consumption and theft was an illusion caused by alcohol consumption's correlation with another variable which was more directly correlated with theft. Patterns of alcohol consumption and of theft could both be related to larger cultural patterns or traditions, of course, but the correlation between theft rates at the beginning and at the end of the period does not suggest the importance of a tradition of delinquency; if traditions of theft were important determinants of theft rates one would expect levels of theft at the beginning of the century to be highly correlated with those at the end of the century, but in fact the coefficient was only $r=0.21$. The relationship between theft and alcohol consumption, in other words, may be only an illusion, caused by a close relationship between these phenomena and other causative variables such as cultural traditions, economic well-being, or alienation which is absent or imperfectly measured in this set of indexes, but this cannot be proved with these variables. The relationship between theft and alcohol cannot be explained away easily.

Nevertheless it can be shown that the relationships between theft and other variables in the groups were not the result of the latter acting upon theft by way of alcohol consumption. When alcohol consumption is held constant, correlations between theft and the other main variables remain high. Thus the correlation between urbanism and alcohol, for example, is not the result of higher alcohol consumption in cities than in the countryside. Among the variables in this group, alcohol is truly independent.

BIBLIOGRAPHY

The following is a selected bibliography. Many sources dealing with secondary aspects of the problem or more general background works, some of which have been cited in the notes, are not included. This material may be found in a number of other bibliographies, including those in my Ph.D. dissertation, on file at Rutgers University; in Peter N. Stearns, *European Society in Upheaval: Social History Since 1750* (2nd ed. rev., New York, 1975); and in David S. Landes, 'Technological Change and Development in Western Europe, 1750-1914' in *The Cambridge Economic History of Europe*, Vol. VI Part I, (Cambridge, England, 1965).

Secondary Sources: Discussions of Crime and Related Issues

Books

Aschaffenburg, Gustav, *Crime and its Repression*, translated by Adalbert Albrecht (Boston, 1913).

Bonger, William Adrian, *Criminality and Economic Conditions*, translated by Henry P. Horton (New York, 1967).

Burchardt, Hans Hermann, *Kriminalität in Stadt und Land* (Berlin, 1936).

Caullet, Paul *Cours de police administrative et judiciaire* (Paris, 1928).

Chen, Yak-Yon, *Etudes statistiques sur la criminalité en France de 1895 à 1930* (Paris, 1937).

Chevalier, Louis, *Classes laborieuses et classes dangereuses* (Paris, 1958).

Clinard, Marshall B. (ed.), *Anomie and Deviant Behavior* (New York, 1964).

Coser, Lewis, *The Functions of Social Conflict* (New York, 1964).

Cressy, Donald R., and Ward, David A., *Delinquency, Crime, and Social Process* (New York, 1969).

Douglas, Jack D., *The Social Meaning of Suicide* (Princeton, 1967).

Durkheim, Emile, *Suicide: A Study in Sociology* (New York, 1951).

Esmein, A., *Histoire de la procédure criminelle en France* (Paris, 1881).

Exner, Franz, *Studien über die Stratzumesungspraxis der deutschen Gerichte* (Leipzig, 1931).

Fosdick, Raymond B., *European Police Systems* (New York, 1915).

Fuld, L., *Der Einfluss der Lebensmittelpreise auf die Bewegung der strafbaren Handlungen* (Mainz, 1881).

Guerry, A.M., *Essai sur la statistique morale de la France* (Paris, 1833).

Gurr, Ted Robert, *Why Men Rebel* (Princeton, 1971).

Henry, Andrew F., and Short, James F., Jr., *Suicide and Homicide: Some Economic, Sociological and Psychological Aspects of Aggression* (New York, 1968).

Hood, Roger, and Sparks, Richard, *Key Issues in Criminology* (New York, 1970).

Joachim, Eduard, *Konjunktur und Kriminalität* (Offenburg, 1933).

Joly, Henri, *La France criminelle* (Paris, 1889).

Lauriot, André, *La police à Paris et en province* (Paris, 1924).

Le Clère, Marcel, *Histoire de la police* (Paris, 1947 and 1964).

Liepmann, Moritz, *Krieg und Kriminalität in Deutschland* (Stuttgart, 1930).

McClintock, F.H. and Avison, N. Howard, *Crime in England and Wales* (London, 1968).

McLennan, Barbara N., *Crime in Urban Society* (New York, 1970).

Macé, G., *Un joli monde* (Paris, 1887).

——, *Le service de la Sureté* (Paris, 1884).

Mannheim, Hermann, *Comparative Criminology* (Boston, 1965).

Mayr, Georg von, *Statistik und Gesellschaftslehe*, Vol. 3: *Moralstatistik mit Einschluss der Kriminalstatistik* (Tübingen, 1917).

Mays, John Barron, *Crime and the Social Structure* (London, 1963).

Oettingen, Alexander von, *Die Moralstatistik in ihrer Bedeutung für eine Socialethik* (Erlangen, 1882).

Reckless, Walter G., *The Crime Problem*, 3rd ed. (New York, 1961).

Savitz, Leonard, *Dilemmas in Criminology* (NewYork, 1967).

Say Horace, *Etudes sur l'administration de Paris et du département de la Seine* (Paris, 1846).

Schnapper-Arndt, Gottlieb, *Sozialstatistik* (Leipzig, 1908).

Sellin, J. Thorsten, *et al., A Bibliographic Manual for the Student of Criminology* (New York, 1965).

——, and Wolfgang, Marvin E., *The Measure of Delinquency* (New York, 1964).

—-, *Research Memorandum on Crime in the Depression*, Social Science Research Council Bulletin 27 (New York, 1937).

Seuffert, Hermann, and Friedberg, E., *Untersuchungen über die örtliche Verteilung der Verbrechen im deutschen Reich*, in *Strafrechliche Abhandlungen*, Heft 75 (Breslau, 1906).

Shaw, Clifford R., and McKay, Henry D., *Juvenile Delinquency and Urban Areas* (Chicago, 1942).

Shields, J.V.M., and Duncan, Judith, *The State of Crime in Scotland*

(London, 1964).

Stanciu, V.V., *La criminalité à Paris* (Paris, 1968).

Sutherland, Edwin H., *White-collar Crime* (New York, 1950).

——, and Cressey, Donald R., *Principles of Criminology*, 7th ed. (New York, 1966).

Szabo, Denis, *Crimes et villes: Etudes statistiques de la criminalité urbaine et rurale en France et en Belgique* (Paris, 1960).

——, *Les delits impoursuivis, essais, etc.* (Lyon, Paris, 1895).

Tarde, G., *La criminalite comparée*, 8th ed. (Paris, 1924).

Thomas, Dorothy S., *Social Aspects of the Business Cycle* (London, 1925).

Tobias, J.J., *Urban Crime in Victorian England* (New York, 1972).

Vidal, G., *Considérations sur l'état actuel de la criminalité en France* (Paris 1904).

Vold, George B., *Theoretical Criminology* (New York, 1958).

Wolfgang, Marvin F., *Patterns in Criminal Homicide* (Philadelphia, 1958).

Wolfgang, Marvin E. (ed.), *Studies in Homicide* (New York, 1967).

Wrights, Erik Olin, *The Politics of Punishment: A Critical Analysis of Prisons in America* (New York, 1973).

Articles, Essays

Arnold, F. Ch., 'Zur Kriminalstatistik', *Der Gerichtssaal* 9 Jg., Vol. 2 (1857), pp. 232-7.

Aschrott, P.F., 'Dreissig Jahre deutscher Kriminalstatistik', *Zeitschrift für die gesamte Strafrechtswissenschaft*, 35 (1914), pp. 507 ff.

Baur, E.J., 'Statistical Indexes of the Social Aspects of Countries', *Social Forces*, 33 (October 1954), pp. 64-75.

Beattie, Ronald H., 'Sources of Criminal Statistics', *Annals of the American Academy of Political and Social Science*, 217 (1941), pp. 19-28.

Bemmeln, J.M. van, 'The Constancy of Crime', *British Journal of Delinquency*, 2 (1952), pp. 208-28.

Bogen, David, 'Juvenile Delinquency and Economic Trend', *American Sociological Review*, 9 (April 1944), pp. 178-84.

Christiansen, Karl O., 'Industrialization and Urbanization in relation to Crime and Juvenile Delinquency', *International Review of Criminal Policy*, 16 (October 1960), pp. 3-8.

Clinard, Marshall, B., 'The Process of Urbanization and Criminal Behavior: A Study of Culture Conflicts', *American Journal of Sociology*, 48 (September 1942), pp. 302-13.

— —, 'Rural Criminal Offenders', *American Journal of Sociology*, 50 (July 1944), pp. 38-50.

Davies, James C., 'The J-Curve of Rising and Declining Satisfaction as a Cause of Some Great Revolutions and a Contained Rebellion', in Hugh Davis Graham and Ted Robert Gurr (eds.), *Violence in America* (New York, 1969), pp. 671-709.

Ekelund, Erik, 'Criminal Statistics: The Volume of Crime', *Journal of Criminal Law and Criminology* 32 (1942), pp. 540-7.

Gatrell, V.A.C., and Hadden, T.B., 'Criminal Statistics and their Interpreation', in E.A. Wrigley (ed.), *Nineteenth Century Society: Essays in the Use of Quantitative Methods for the Study of Social Data*, (Cambridge (England), 1972), pp. 336-96.

Graham, Fred P., 'A Contemporary History of American Crime', in Hugh Davis Graham and Ted Robert Gurr (eds.), *Violence in America* (New York, 1969), pp. 460-78.

Grunhut, M., 'Statistics in Criminology', *Journal of the Royal Statistical Society*, Series A, Vol. CXIV (1951), pp. 139-57.

Hackney, Sheldon, 'Southern Violence' in Hugh Davis Graham and Ted Robert Gurr (eds.), *Violence in America* (New York, 1969), pp. 479-500.

Hentig, Hans von, 'Der kriminelle Aspekt von Stadt und Land', *Monatsschrift für Kriminalpsychologie*, 23 (July 1932), pp. 435-6.

Hobbs, Albert H., 'Relationship between Criminality and Economic Conditions', *Journal of Criminal Law and Criminology*, 34 (May 1943), pp. 5-10.

Hoegel, H., 'Die Grenzen der Kriminalstatistik', *Statistische Monatsschrift*, Neue Folge XII (1907), pp. 345 ff, 387 ff, 449 ff.

Körner, 'Die Neusten Publikationen über die Kriminalität in Preussen', *Jahrbücher für Nationalökonomie und Statistik*, Neue Folge XIII (1886), pp. 225-38.

Kruger, Kurt, 'Die Entwicklung der Kriminalität im deutschen Reich, 1882-1910', *Jahrbücher für Nationalökonomie und Statistik*, III Folge, vol. 47 (1914), pp. 658-75.

Le Clère, Marcel 'L'indice criminel de la France', *Revue de Science Criminelle et de Droit Pénal Comparé* (January-March 1959).

Lentz, William P., 'Rural Urban Differentials and Juvenile Delinquency', *Journal of Criminal Law, Criminology and Police Science*, 47 (September-October 1956), pp. 331-9.

MacDonald, Arthur, 'Criminal Statistics in Germany, France and England', *Journal of Criminal Law and Criminology*, 1, Part II (1910), pp. 59-70.

Mack, Raymond W., and Snyder, Richard C., 'The Analysis of Social
    Conflict — Toward an Overview and Synthesis', *Journal of Conflict
    Resolution*, 1 (June 1957), pp. 212-48.
Morrison, W.D., 'The Interpretation of Criminal Statistics', *Journal of
    the Royal Statistical Society*, 60 (1897), pp. 1 ff.
Müller, Heinrich, 'Untersuchungen über die Bewegung der Kriminalität
    in ihrem Zusammenhang mit dem wirtschaftlichen Verhältnissen',
    Dissertation, Halle a. S., 1899.
Ogburn, W.F., 'The Fluctuations of Business as Social Forces', *Social
    Forces*, 1 (January 1923), pp. 73-8.
Parratt, Spencer D., 'How Effective is a Police Department', *Annals of
    the American Academy of Political and Social Science*, 199
    (September 1938), pp. 153-64.
Phelps, H.A., 'Cycles of Crime', *Journal of Criminal Law and Crimino-
    logy*, 20 (May-June 1929), pp. 107-21.
Potter, Ellen C., 'Spectacular Aspects of Crime in Relation to the Crime
    Wave', *Annals of the American Academy of Political and Social
    Science*, 125 (May 1926), pp. 1-19.
Powell, Elwin H., 'Crime as a Function of Anomie', *Journal of Criminal
    Law, Criminology and Police Science*, 57 (June 1966), pp. 161-71.
Radzinowicz, L., 'A Note on Methods of Establishing the Connexion
    between Economic Conditions and Crime', *Sociological Review*, 31
    July 1939), pp. 260-80.
——, 'The Influence of Economic Conditions on Crime', *Sociological
    Review*, 33 (January-May 1941), pp. 1-36, 139-53.
Reinemann, J.O., 'Juvenile Delinquency in Philadelphia and Economic
    Trends', *Temple University Law Quarterly*, 20 (April 1947), pp.
    576-83.
Ridke, Ronald G., 'Discontent and Economic Growth', *Economic
    Development and Cultural Change*, 11 (October 1962), pp. 1-15.
Roesner, Ernst, 'Polizeistatistik', in *Handwörterbuch der Kriminologie
    und der anderem strafrechtlichen Hilfswissenschaften* 2 (Berlin,
    1933), pp. 348-80.
Scheel, H. von, 'Kriminalstatistik', in *Handwörterbuch der Staatswissen-
    schaften*, 3 Auflage 6 vols. (Jena, 1910), pp. 246-53.
Sellin, J. Thorsten, 'The Significance of Records of Crime', *Law
    Quarterly Review*, 67 (1951), pp. 489-504.
Shaw, Van B., 'Relationship between Crime Rates and Certain Popula-
    tion Characteristics in Minnesota Counties', *Journal of Criminal Law
    and Criminology*, 40 (May-June 1949), pp. 43-9.
Short, James F., Jr., 'An Investigation of the Relation Between Crime

and Business Cycles', Ph.D. dissertation, University of Chicago, 1951.
——, 'A Social Aspect of the Business Cycle Re-examined: Crimes',
    Research Studies of the College of Washington, 20 (1952), pp.
    36-41.
Siefrieda, 'Ortsüblicher Tagelohn und Kriminalität in Preussen', *Die
    Neue Zeit*, 1, Jg. 24 (1905/6), pp. 636-8.
Silver, Alan, 'The Demand for Order in Civil Society: A Review of
    Some Themes in the History of Urban Crime, Police and Riot', in
    David J. Bordua, *The Police: Six Sociological Essays*, (New York,
    1967).
Stursberg, Hugo, *Die Zunahme der Vergehen und Verbrechen und ihre
    Ursachen* (Düsseldorf, 1879).
Taft, Donald R., 'Testing the Selective Influence of Areas of Delin-
    quency', *American Journal of Sociology*, 38 (March 1933), pp.
    699-712.
Tilly, Charles, 'Collective Violence in European Perspective', in Hugh
    Davis Graham and Ted Robert Gurr (eds.), *Violence in America*
    (New York, 1969), pp. 4-42.
——, 'How Protest Modernised in France 1845-1855', in William O.
    Aydelotte, Allan G. Bogue and Robert William Fogel (eds.), *The
    Dimensions of Quantitative Research in History* (Princeton, 1972),
    pp. 192-255.
Tilly, Charles; Tilly, Louise; and Tilly, Richard, *The Rebellious Century:
    1830-1930* (Cambridge, 1975).
Tilly, Richard, 'Popular Disorders in Nineteenth-Century Germany: A
    Preliminary Survey', *Journal of Social History*, 4 (Fall 1970), pp. 1-40.
Tönnies, F., 'Das Verbrechen als soziale Erscheinung', *Archiv für
    soziale Gesetzgebung und Statistik*, 8 (1895), pp. 392 ff.
Vislock-Young, Pauline, 'Urbanization as a Factor in Juvenile Delin-
    quency', *American Sociological Society*, 24 (May 1930), pp. 162-6.
Vold, George B., 'Crime in City and Country Areas', *Annals of the
    American Academy of Political and Social Science*, 217 (September
    1941), pp. 38-45.
Warner, S.B., 'Crimes Known to the Police — An Index of Crime',
    Harvard Law Review, 45 (December 1931), pp. 307-34.
Weisz, B., 'Ueber einige wirtschaftliche und moralische Wirkungen
    hoher Getreidepreise', *Jahrbücher für Nationalökonomie und
    Statistik*, Neue Folge 3 (1881), pp. 80-90.
Winslow, Emma A., 'Relationships between Employment and Crime
    Fluctuations as shown by Massachusetts Statistics', *Report on the
    Causes of Crime, National Commission on Law Enforcement*, No. 13,

Vol. 1 (Washington, 1937).

Wolfgang, Marvin E., 'Urban Crime', in James Q. Wilson (ed.), *The Metropolitan Enigma* (Cambridge, Mass., 1968), pp. 246-81.

Wolfgang, Marvin E., and Strohm, Rolf, 'The Relationship between Alcohol and Criminal Homicide', *Quarterly Journal of Studies on Alcohol*, 17 (1956), pp. 411-25.

Woytinsky, W., 'Lebensmittlepreise.Beschäftigundsgrad und Kriminalität', *Archiv für Sozialwissenschaft und Sozialpolitik*, Vol. 61, Heft 3, (Tübingen, 1929), pp. 21-62.

Yvernès, M., 'La Justice en France de 1881 à 1900', *Journal de la Société de Statistique de Paris* (1903).

Zahn, F., 'Aufgaben und Leistungen der Polizeistatistik', in *Allgemeines Statistisches Archiv* 9, Heft 2/3 (Munich, 1915), pp. 364-96.

Primary Sources: Crime Statistics

Crime statistics are also included in many of the works previously cited, and sources of statistics for other areas and periods are listed in Zehr, 'Patterns of Crime', Appendix and Bibliography.

France: Published

Compte général de l'administration de la justice criminelle en France (1827-1910), Paris.

Germany: Published

Listed in alphabetical order by locality.

Geschäftsbericht des grossherzoglich badischen Ministeriums des Innern für die Jahre 1897 bis 1905, Vol. 1 (Karlsruhe, 1907).

'Regierungs-Blatt' [Baden] (1831 to 1841).

Statistisches Jahrbuch für des Grossherzogtum Baden (1882-1914) (Karlsruhe).

Beiträge zur Statistik des Königreichs Bayern, Vols. II, III, VII, VIII, IX, XIII, XV, XVII (Munich, 1853-65).

Mayr, Georg von, *Statistik der Gerichtlichen Polizei im Königreiche Bayern und in eingen anderen Landern*, XVI Heft: *Beiträge zur Statistik des Königreiches Bayern* (Munich, 1867).

Bericht über die Verwaltung und den Stand der Gemeindeangelegenheiten der Stadt Bonn für das Etatsjahr ... [1845, 1847-51, 1869-1913] (Bonn).

Statistisches Jahrbuch der Stadt Berlin I-XXXIII (Berlin).

Verwaltungs-Bericht der Stadt Bochum (1864-1909) (Bochum).

Statistik des Kreises Bochum (1865-1880) (Bochum).

Statistische Datem über die Stadt Breslau, Vol. 1913 (Breslau).

Verwaltungs-Bericht des Magistrats der Königlichen Haupt- und Residenzstadt Breslau (1877-1891) (Breslau).

Bericht über die Verwaltung und den Stand des Gemeindeangelegenheiten der Fabrik und Handelstadt Chemnitz (1893, 1900-1910) (Chemnitz).

Bericht über den Stand und die Verwaltung der Gemeindeangelegenheiten der Stadt Duisberg (1863 to 1912/14) (Duisberg).

Bericht über den Stand und die Verwaltung der Gemeinde-Angelegenheiten der Stadt Düsseldorf (1878-1912) (Düsseldorf).

Jahresbericht des Statistischen Amts der Stadt Düsseldorf (1902-1914) (Düsseldorf).

Bericht über den Stand und die Verwaltung der Gemeindeangelegenheiten der Stadtgemeinde Merscheid (1865, 1868, 1874, 1876, 1878, 1890) (Ohligs).

Bericht über die Verwaltung und den Stand der Gemeindeangelegenheiten der Stadt Mülheim-am-Rhein (1875-1911) (Mülheim-am-Rhein).

Statistisches Jahrbuch der Stadt Nürnberg, Vol. II and Vol. V (Nürnberg, 1910 and 1914).

Verwaltungsbericht der Stadt Nürnberg (1896-1910) (Nürnberg).

Bericht über die Verwaltung und den Stand der Gemeinde-Angelegenheiten der Stadt Oberhausen, Rheinland (1862-1906) (Oberhausen).

Bericht über die Verwaltung und den Stand der Gemeinde-Angelegenheiten der Stadt Ohligs für den Zeitraum vom 1 April 1911 bis 31 Marz 1922 (Ohligs, 1927).

Illing, J., 'Die Zahlen der Kriminalität in Preussen für 1854 bis 1884', *Zeitschrift des Königlich-Preussischen Statistischen Bureaus*, Jg. 25 (1885), pp. 1 ff.

Starke, W., *Verbrechen und Verbrecher in Preussen 1854-78. (Berlin, 1884).*

Statistische Handbuch für den Preussischen Staat, Vols. I-IV (Berlin, 1888-1903).

Statistische Jahrbuch für den Preussischen Staat (1903-13) (Berlin).

Statistische Jahrbuch deutscher Städte, Vols. I-XX (Breslau).

Statisk des deutschen Reichs, Neue Folge 1-149 (1884-1903), without prefix 150- (1903-) (Berlin). Crime Statistics: NF 8, 13, 18, 23, 30, 37, 45, 52, 58, 64, 71, 77, 83, 89, 95, 120, 126, 132, 139, 146, 155, 162, 169, 176, 185, 193, 228, 237, 247, 257, 267, 272.

Statistische Monatsberichte der Stadt Stuttgart im Auftrag der Bürger-

lichen Kollegien, 1-4 Jg (Stuttgart, 1896-1900).

Statistische Jahrbuch der Stadt Stuttgart (1900, 1901, 1902, 1902-13)
(Stuttgart).

'Regierungs-Blatt für das Königreich Württemberg' (1834-1848)
(Stuttgart).

Staatsanzeiger für Württemberg (1849-1913) (Stuttgart).

Statistische Handbuch für das Königreich Württemberg (1908-1910)
(Stuttgart).

Württembergische Jahrbücher für Statistik und Landeskunde (1889-
1912) (Stuttgart).

Germany: Archival
Listed in alphabetical order by locality.

Stadtarchiv Bochum Zeitungsberichte, 'Statistische Nachrichten'
(Landkreis Bochum, 1897-1904).

Staatsarchiv Münster, Kreis Bochum 51^{I-V}, 'Zeitungsberichte'
(Landkreis Bochum, 1842-1881).

Stadtarchiv Duisberg, Polizeiakten 301/172, 'Verbrechen und Vergeben'
(1903-1907, 1909-1911).

Stadtarchiv Düsseldorf, Aktenbanden III 4588-III 4603, 'Zeitungsberichte' (Düsseldorf, 1878-1913).

Hauptstaatarchiv Stuttgart E151cII No 429, 'Königliches Landjägercorps: Uebersicht über die Festnahmen und Anzeigen [1900-1913]'
(Württemberg).

INDEX